Systematic discography

Systematic discography

LEWIS FOREMAN

LINNET BOOKS & CLIVE BINGLEY

Library of Congress Cataloging in Publication Data

Foreman, Lewis.
    Systematic discography.

    Bibliography: p
    1. Cataloging of phonorecords.   I. Title.
Z695.715.F67   025.3'4'8   74-8463
ISBN 0–208–01197–8

FIRST PUBLISHED 1974 BY CLIVE BINGLEY LTD
THIS EDITION SIMULTANEOUSLY PUBLISHED IN THE USA BY
LINNET BOOKS, AN IMPRINT OF THE SHOE STRING PRESS INC
995 SHERMAN AVENUE HAMDEN CONNECTICUT 06514
PRINTED IN GREAT BRITAIN
COPYRIGHT © LEWIS FOREMAN 1974
ALL RIGHTS RESERVED

CONTENTS

INTRODUCTION

No one has previously attempted to produce a comprehensive guide to the compilation of discographies. However, in reality there are no specific rules to follow, only the example of those already in the field, and the dictates of the material being catalogued.

In this study, therefore, I have not attempted to lay down hard and fast rules. Instead I have briefly sketched the background of the materials that are being catalogued by discographers and the reasons for wanting to make such listings, and then shown the problems that arise. The variety of possible solutions that have been produced to these problems are themselves the best stimulus to solving any future problem. There is only one way to achieve any skill in discography, and that is by collecting the recordings in one's area of interest, so that the materials being discussed are known intimately, and then base one's discography on this material.

The techniques at present being used have been developed by enthusiastic amateurs over the last forty years. This is a field in which the major expertise is held by people who indulge it as a hobby. Professional librarians are only now finding it necessary to develop cataloguing codes and agreed formats for dealing with recorded sound, but they still have much to learn from what has gone before.

This book is aimed at several different groups of reader. Firstly it is intended as a textbook for the professional librarian, some of whom have hitherto perhaps tended to undervalue recordings as materials. Secondly, it is intended as a guide to all those amateur discographers of the earlier part of the present century. Finally, it is intended as a guide to the ordinary record collector who wants to catalogue his collection, or to document a specialist interest, and who needs some guide to focussing his thoughts onto the problems which are likely to confront him.

If it also persuades the authors and publishers of books on music, and other fields in which recordings are valuable sources, that all their publications aspiring to scholarship must have a discography if their bibliographical apparatus is to achieve its potential value to users, then the author will be more than satisfied.

It was originally intended to include an extended bibliography of discographies of 'serious' music. However, the bibliography grew so large that it had to be detached from the text and published separately. It may often be found useful in conjunction with the present text. (*Discographies: a bibliography*. Triad Press, 1973.)

ACKNOWLEDGEMENTS
Acknowledgement is made to all the authors and publishers of material quoted: the sources are shown in the text in full or by reference to the bibliography.

I would particularly like to thank for the more extended quotations and examples, Stuart Hall and the BBC for the use of unpublished material, John Stratton, John R T Davies and J Dennis, F F Clough, the Rev G J Cuming and Sidgwick & Jackson for all the material from WERM, and Clough and Cuming for other material of theirs, and also Sidgwick & Jackson for the material from BAUER.

To those who gave up time in order to help special thanks are due; to Stanley Day for allowing an interview, Sally Tarshish for translating the introduction to *Celletti* even though little of it has actually appeared in print, to William Schwann for writing with details of his *Schwann record & tape guide,* to Patrick Saul and the BIRS for assistance with material originating from *Recorded Sound* and its predecessor, to Jerrold Northrup Moore for discussing his *Elgar Discography,* and finally to R D Darrell who effectively started it all and whose letters and permission to use his material have been greatly appreciated.

Finally Malcolm Walker, Anthony Pollard, Bob Scoales and Tony Curwen read the book in proof and made valuable suggestions, and Edward Sargent provided much valuable information about the American scene.

LEWIS FOREMAN

Cononbury, July 1973
Aberystwyth, April 1974

I

SOUND RECORDING AND ITS PLACE IN THE DOCUMENTATION OF TWENTIETH CENTURY HISTORY

In 1877, Charles Cros, a dilettante French scientist, wrote a paper entitled *Procédé d'enregistrement et de reproduction des phénomènes perçus par l'ouïe,* in which he described a process for sound recording on a disc record, the sound being carried in laterally and vertically modulated grooves. The development of sound recording earlier in the nineteenth century had not been due to lack of technology, but largely because scientists such as Cros experimenting on sound and wave theory never seem to have had an inkling of the possibilities inherent in a practical application of their pure researches. It took the inventive genius of Edison to provide the practical basis of the record as it is known today, and in showing that it could work, to offer the incentive for other research and development.

As a byproduct, while experimenting with a high speed telegraph relay Edison produced the tinfoil cylinder phonograph. This was in November 1877. The results obtained appear to have exceeded Edison's expectations, and some 500 examples of the machine were produced in 1878, although no contemporary recordings have been traced as surviving. At this stage, of course, there was no production of material to play on the machine: it was just a scientific curiosity, which recorded and played—very primitively—on the same machine. Edison's attention was soon diverted into what appeared to be more profitable channels, the problems of the development of the incandescent lamp and electrical power systems.

The development of an improved recording system was continued by Alexander Graham Bell, Chichester Bell and C S Tainter, utilising the idea of wax as a medium for carrying the sound. Eventually a practicable cylinder dictating-machine was produced and marketed in 1885.

Experimentation then moved to problems of manufacture: a method for mass producing the recordings made on fragile wax cylinders. This ultimately meant the demise of the cylinder, once the concept of a flat disc as the recording surface had been developed. The development of the lateral disc recording by Emile Berliner was

9

1*

probably the most important development of all for the modern recording industry. While wax remained necessary for making the recording, the preparation of a metal master from the original wax and the ability to press large quantities in shellac laid the foundation of the modern industry.

Developments in methods of making the turntable revolve at constant speed, and refinements in the actual acoustic amplification of the sound, with sound boxes and horns of various designs, were the only real areas of extension of the art until the introduction of electrical recording through microphones in 1924.

The slump in the late 'twenties and early 'thirties was probably the major dampening factor in the expansion of what was at the time a luxury-goods industry. In particular this prevented the early development of the long playing record. The depression of the early 'thirties was an important factor in making for the present shape of the industry. In the years before 1930—the period following the introduction of electrical recording—there was something of a boom in the industry and high profits encouraged the entry of several new firms. The effect was to flood the market, so that new records sold for as little as a shilling.

' The drastic shrinkage of the market brought about by the depression put all but the strongest firms out of business. The amalgamation between HMV and Columbia had taken place in the spring of 1931.'[15]

Since the second world war, massive technical developments have resulted in a phenomenal expansion of material from all sources. Of these, the improvement in sound quality, of which the Decca *ffrr* system was a portent, has been the most important. The development of the LP record as a commercial proposition in 1948, followed by the stereo record in 1958, resulted in a unique expansion in the recorded repertoire. The volume of commercially recorded material is phenomenally large, though not quite as comprehensive as some advertising would have one believe. Equally important was the development of the tape recorder. Not only are domestic users able to preserve broadcast material for their own use in very high sound quality, but archives have expanded accordingly. Total documentation of some subjects begins to be a possibility for the historian.

ETHNOMUSICOLOGY

The history of sound recording as a serious medium dates back to the 1890s. It is in the field of what is now known as ethnomusicology that this new technical development was first recognised as a valuable research tool.

The first phonograms of exotic music were made by Dr Walter Fewkes in 1889 from the singing of Passamaquoddy and Zuñi Indians in the USA. (See Kunst, Jaap: *Ethnomusicology*, The Hague, Martinus Nijhoff, 1969.) These records were passed on for analysis and elaboration to Dr B I Gilman of Harvard University, and this led to the publication of his study *Zuni melodies (Journal of American archaeology and ethnology* I 1891) which has served as an example to many later treatises based on recorded material.

The development of the medium quickly gave rise to the establishment of collections of recordings, although the early promise in one particular field has taken a long time to become accepted in other fields. In 1899 the Vienna Academy of Science defined the state *Phonothèque*. But it was the establishment of the Berlin Phonogramm-Archiv, by the famous psychologist Carl Stumpf, that gave the impetus to the establishment of such collections.

Stumpf first recorded the court orchestra of Siam when it visited Berlin in 1900. These cylinder recordings were deposited in the Psychological Institute of Berlin University and during the ensuing years other recordings were deposited by travellers and ethnologists, until the Phonogramm-Archiv was formed in 1904. The collection quickly expanded, by making Edison phonographs available to field workers and by exchanging recordings with other institutions that had started collections elsewhere in the world. In order to duplicate recordings for this purpose, electrotype matrices were made, from which copies were made. During March and April 1901, Sir Charles Baldwin Spencer recorded aboriginal songs in Australia, pre-dating Australia's most famous field recordist, Percy Grainger, by several years.

Among composers who engaged in collecting folk songs were Bartok and Kodaly in Hungary and Eastern Europe and Percy Grainger in England and Scandinavia. ' With the aid of the same type of machine, the wax cylinder phonograph, both (*ie* Grainger and Bartok) independently collected folk songs in their respective countries in 1905 and, apparently unaware of each other's work, published their first findings one year later.' (Slattery, Thomas C: *The wind music of Percy Aldridge Grainger*, University of Iowa, unpublished PHD thesis, 1967, p 26-27.)

Such collecting not only gave the composers authentic folk-materials which was reflected in their composed music, but quickly assembled a sizeable corpus of material which had been collected and documented by some of the most creative and brilliant musical minds of their time. Thus in 1912 Bartok could write: 'Up to now I have handed in nearly 1000 phonograph cylinder recordings to the Ethnographic Museum in Budapest'.

In 1922, 1925, and 1927, with the aid of Grainger's wax cylinder phonograph, Grainger and Tang Kristensen collected nearly two hundred folk songs of the Jutland peninsula.

WILDLIFE RECORDINGS

The name of Ludwig Koch is so familiar today that it comes as a surprise to learn that as early as 1889 he had made a recording of the song of the Indian Shama, and a disc copy of the original wax cylinder is still preserved in the BBC Sound Archive. However, early recordings tended to be somewhat gimmicky, including human impersonations of bird-song, and later Beatrice Harrison's famous cello solo to a background of the nightingale's song.

In 1898, reference had been made to a recording of bird song in a scientific paper, indicating that the new science became respectable in the scientific field almost as soon as it had in anthropology.

The development of wildlife recording has owed a lot to the impetus given to it by the BBC's natural history unit, and more recently the establishment of the British Library of Wildlife Sound (BLOWS).

MUSIC AND SPEECH

Soon after the perfection of the phonograph, many famous people made recordings, a number of which have survived. Such famous nineteenth century names as Tennyson (see discography in *Bulletin of the BIRS* Winter 1956 p 2-5), Gladstone, Florence Nightingale and Sir Arthur Sullivan, perpetuated their voices in this way. (These early recordings are reproduced on Argo's excellent sound history of the gramophone 'The wonder of the age' Argo ZPR 122-3.)

Once the flat disc could be mass-produced (by the late 1890s) something of a scramble began as different companies sought to secure the services of singers, and, to a lesser extent, instrumentalists, to make recordings. A Russian soprano Maria Michailova was among the first to record commercially, and to make a reputation thereby that she would not have otherwise enjoyed. But it was in the early years of the twentieth century that the major expansion was made, and it is from this period that the earliest recordings of acceptable quality are still extant. It must be admitted that to the modern ear they are primitive in sound quality, but nevertheless remain valuable historical documents. Certainly it is fortunate that the singing voice reproduces remarkably faithfully from such old recordings, and it is in this period that the principal discoveries of recorded material known from catalogues and archives, but at present unknown in extant copies, may yet be made.

The first complete opera recording was of Verdi's *Ernani* on 40 single sided Italian HMVs (in 1903), and the first complete symphony, Beethoven's *Fifth* (under Nikisch), in 1913 040784/91). The dating of this particular recording appears to be in doubt. In the Nikisch discography in *Recorded sound* (Autumn 1961, p 114-115) it is dated as 1913. However, in *The gramophone jubilee book,*[20] it is dated as 1913 on p 38 and 1909 on p 18. The first British symphony on disc was McEwen's *Solway*, recorded by Vocalion in 1923, (J04043 J04041/3) and in America it was Roy Harris's *Symphony 1933* recorded by American Columbia (68183/6D) in the year of its composition.

By 1910 there was scarcely a singer of any reputation who had not made records, and artists of Caruso's stature could command large fees. Instrumental music began to appear before the first world war, but the expansion of the repertoire in that direction, and also as far as orchestral music was concerned, did not occur in any quantity before the end of the war. Once electrical recording became a reality (in 1924) then a quality was achieved that allows one to make a full and realistic assessment of the performance today, based on the sound actually heard, rather than having to make allowances for deficiencies in recording technique. Nevertheless to hear Nikisch and Fried conduct is to gain an insight into a musical tradition stretching back into the nineteenth century; even though questions of balance and actual orchestral *sound* would in no way be represented on the actual disc in any authentic degree, owing to the studio conditions at the time. (See 'In the recording studio' by Stanley Chapple, *Gramophone* December 1928, p 289-291). This is also true of instrumental technique, and particularly singing (see, for example, John Stratton, 'Operatic singing style and the gramophone' *Recorded sound* April-July 1966, 37-68).

The outstanding feature of the 1960s is the advance in techniques for reproducing early records, and in the explosion of LP transfers of 78rpm originals, as well as the sudden discovery and dissemination of previously untapped sources of archival material, unpublished and still preserved. The publication of much of this material is the major achievement of a growing number of small ' pirate ' firms, mainly in the USA, who contravene performing rights regulations with apparent impunity, but make available to those who know where to look undreamed-of treasures—as, for example, the 1934 world premiere of Howard Hanson's opera *Merry mount* (EJS134).

THE GROWTH OF DISCOGRAPHY

Before the second world war, discography originated in the major record companies' very comprehensively arranged lists (see, for example, the HMV list for September 1937), in the beginnings of a jazz discographical tradition in the 1930s, in the publication of a number of guides to the ' best records ', and in the publications of the Gramophone Shop, New York. The latter's *Encyclopedia of the world's best recorded music* second edition (NY, The Gramophone Shop, 1931) was the forerunner of Darrell's *Gramophone Shop encyclopedia of recorded music,* which appeared in 1936 and is colloquially known as *Darrell.*

Thus, it may be seen that before the 1930s the only area where any serious analysis of the existing material was made was in the field of ethnomusicology.

In the 1920s the popular *Home book of opera* underlined the continuing interest in vocal recordings, and provided a basic discographical tool, which with the manufacturers' lists pre-dates the more general compilations which first appeared in the 1930s. Then the seeds were laid for a developing craft of discography, although the final blooming did not come until after the second world war. There is still a vast amount of material to be considered and such guides as *World encyclopedia of recorded music* (WERM) can only be considered as general guides to the available heritage of recorded sound. A truly comprehensive world discography will probably now never be compiled, but through a large number of ad-hoc subject discographies, contributed largely by private collectors (particularly in the vocal field), access to the history of performance in the twentieth century *as it took place* is gradually being made possible. Discography now awaits its Bestermann to give final shape to the work already done.

After the broadcasts in 1972 and 1973 of the BBC's epic sound history of the people of Britain, which was called *The long march of Everyman*, Stuart Hall commented in an additional programme on the BBC's sources. He had the following to say about the *sound* sources:

'The 1950s and early 1960s is the period when Britain becomes a society criss-crossed from end to end by the powerful new means of mass communication. The press and radio, of course, continue and grow: radio received an enormous fillip from the role of the BBC in wartime. To these national communications grids is added, in the 1950s, mass television, first by the BBC monopoly, and then by ITV. The media now play a far more decisive role in communicating an image of social change in one part or segment of the society to another: they offer an image of how social change is affecting Britain *as a whole:* above all, they set the framework within which the national dialogue *about* change is conducted. It therefore seemed to me right not only to touch, incidentally, as I did, on the media as a force for change in the period, but to draw my material, as much as I could, from material which had first been recorded for transmission by the media.

'The great bulk of my extracts were selected, therefore, from the BBC Sound Archives. This now constitutes one of the richest primary sources for the contemporary and future social historian. But it also presents him with new problems. The first is that the historian is often working from documentary extracts which have already been inserted into a programme framework different from his own. The social historian working from written sources knows this problem well. The interviews with mods and rockers, for example, now provide a rich insight into attitudes and styles of the period; but they were prompted, first, by the immediate event of the seaside confrontations at Margate and Clacton.

'Radio and television have only gradually become aware of the rich social documentary material which they dispose of every day. It seems the merest good fortune that an occasional interview—like the one with beatniks living rough at the coast—should have survived—for it was originally transmitted in a daily magazine programme, *Today in the south east*, which uses material like this in every single item that it broadcasts.

'Television and radio archives are cumbersome and costly to store and keep: only the tiniest fraction of their daily output can be reckoned on to survive. They are also far less accessible than ordinary printed sources. This is a problem which historians and broadcasters ought urgently to discuss, for what we are dealing with is nothing more or less than the creation of an entirely new and extraordinarily rich documentary historical source.

' When the social historian makes use of printed and written sources originally intended for other purposes, most of his gains will be "incidental". He will pick up significant clues from what the writer may have assured were mere "asides". But there are few "asides" in radio and television. Media material is very heavily edited indeed, to get exactly the phrase or sentence which most directly bears on the broadcasters' theme.

' What fat or spare there is normally finds itself on to the cutting floor. The mass media tend to go for speed, precision and conciseness-to-the-point-at-issue in any programme. They do not encourage people to "talk themselves into their subject", to use speech freely and flexibly in the slow exploration and articulation of complex experiences and feelings. So, most of my extracts are very brief: often, I desperately wanted to hear what followed or came before—I kept shouting at the tape recorder, "Go on . . .", just as the voice was cut, and moved to another speaker. This is one kind or form of communication, and it is done with great professional skill. But it does not sufficiently allow the speaker to change his mind, change the course of his thoughts in mid-sentence, and start again: yet, these are just the rhythms and movements of speech which most subtly record and document the way history imposes itself on the thinking-feeling-acting subject, and registers itself in the consciousness of Everyman. We must do what we can to preserve this too-frequently forgotten, living history of ordinary people hidden away in the new sources of oral history.' (From the unpublished script, by permission of Stuart Hall and the BBC).

Clearly, collections of speech-recordings are going to become more widespread. The present author's *Archive sound collections: an interim directory* (Aberystwyth, College of Librarianship Wales, 1974), is indicative of the way in which archive recordings of all descriptions are becoming recognised as important source materials. In particular, memorates are being collected on an ever widening scale. It is in the interest of all users of such material to make sure that their cataloguing apparatus is adequate.

II

FACTORS AFFECTING THE
PRESERVATION OF RECORDED MATERIALS

As far as the discographer is concerned, he will want to try to ensure that his discography represents all the available material, and also that the material listed will be preserved. There are two clear problems here: a social one (ownership and location of material), and a technical one (preservation of material by its owners, and the physical durability of the recording medium).

OWNERSHIP

There will normally be no problems in identifying commercially made recordings, although unissued recordings that have been preserved by the company concerned may come to light only through personal contact, from test pressings preserved in the performers' own libraries, or, in the case of 78rpm discs, from studies of manufacturers' numbering systems. The appearance of test pressings in second-hand dealers' lists should always be given special attention. ' Pirate ' recordings, mainly emanating from American sources, often mean that material is available which will not be widely advertised, but only known about by word of mouth or by occasional appearances in a few specialised dealers' lists or stock.

Even though major archives are now collecting on a very large scale, privately held material is of importance. In the 1930s the means became available for the wealthy amateur to make his own disc recordings direct from the radio, and material is still coming to light that has been preserved in this way. Naturally, the family of a given composer—or the composer himself if still alive—is always a good starting point for such information. An appropriate contact may often be obtained from one of the collecting societies, or by inspecting the composer's will at Somerset House (or where ever else held in the case of non-British music), and contacting the executors of the estate. However, the complexities of performing rights legislation should be remembered and such material, particularly when of recent origin, should be treated with circumspection. It is often a rewarding, though frequently frustrating, experience to try to work out which major broadcasts might have been preserved, by searching the pages of *Radio times*, or the British Council's *Monthly music broadsheet*, in which the highlights of British musical activities were listed in retrospect. It is also worth remembering that a recording not preserved in the UK might have been preserved overseas if the broadcast had featured in the BBC Transcription Service, and the original disc or a copy had been included in a private collection. This is particularly true of the United States, where there is a vigorous black market in such things. I have known of a BBC transcription disc of the Havergal Brian *Tenth symphony* and the Simpson *First symphony* fetching $75.00.

TECHNICAL QUESTIONS
Most sound recording media were not primarily designed with preservation in mind, but to produce reasonable quality play-back combined with low cost manufacture. In 1959, Pickett and Lemcoe published the results of their researches into the *Preservation and storage of sound recordings*,[14] and this should remain the starting point of all who are involved in the preservation of sound recordings, although there is now an international working party considering the matter, and our knowledge has grown.

To understand the nature of the material on which the recording is preserved is important. The discographer should be able to exercise his judgment to ensure that he is not merely listing material, but is a vital link—indeed *the* vital link—in the chain that ensures the effective *preservation* as well as the dissemination of the recorded sound. The only widely disseminated discussion of the question of the *nature* of the materials on which recordings are made is the Pickett and Lemcoe report, although in that document there are bibliographies indicating further relevant technical sources.

The question of *crackle* and of the deterioration of the actual record surface of 78rpm discs, owing to fungal action, is important. Although dealt with by Pickett and Lemcoe, it has been considered even more recently by Stratton (*Recorded sound* July 1970, p 655-659) to whom I am indebted for the following extract from his article on the subject:

' From the documentary point of view it is appalling the amount of filtering that has been used in large numbers of LPs from 78 originals. And it is the big companies that have been the chief offenders. They generally seem prepared to make any sacrifice to eliminate crackle and coarseness of surface in the original master. The record critics too have often (though I am glad to say not always) been permissive about this practice. Of course one must try to understand that the big companies, and to some extent the critics too, must think in terms of a broad market. There are so many people for whom a silent background is a pre-condition of enjoyable listening. Moreover in fairness to the big companies it should be said that at least some of their transfers of old 78s have been remarkably good. In America Columbia (CBS), for instance, for their Odyssey series have done some astonishing work. Also the EMI group, though in my opinion *their* results are rather uneven even within the confines of such prestige issues as the Great Recordings and Golden Voices series.

' Both Columbia and EMI, it is important to note, have had the advantage, at times, of working from copies of the 78s freshly struck from the masters, or else metal positives. And on such occasions, of course, the crackle problem has simply not arisen.

' It is highly instructive to make some simultaneous comparisons— with wide-range equipment—between original 78s and the LP transfers. What a joy to hear Walter Widdop (on EMI's HQM1164) without a hailstorm background. And even with the grain of the original masters (as distinct from *crackle*) almost eliminated, the voice comes through entirely faithful to the original records. One would expect the Heddle Nash (HQM1089) to be just as good, especially as many of the recordings date from a decade and a half and more later than Widdop's. Likewise the latest Bjoerling transfer (HQM1190). But not so. There is indeed no background noise to distress, however altogether too much of the lustre and glow, the richness and excitement, of these other two voices has been filtered away. Strange that Widdop's voice comes through so well. Perhaps it is a matter of the differences of harmonic structure of the voices? Without direct comparison with the original 78s you might well not guess that there are these discrepancies in the transfers to LP. Everything always sounds so lovely and smooth.

' The mere fact of silent surfaces can be very deceptive. And conversely, many people suppose that *crackle* and an audible surface is tantamount to a distorted and inferior image of the sound recorded.

' The broad public (and even some critics) may be taken in, and the larger record companies may go along happily producing beautiful quiet LPs that murder the originals. But from the documentary point of view this won't do. What is wanted for archives and other more or less permanent collections is the most faithful mirror possible of the originals. Though considering what excellent results EMI and others have from time to time achieved, I think one ought not to be altogether opposed to a certain amount of judicious filtering of the texture of the original 78 masters, and as well to re-balancing of the harmonic structure of the sound where the harmonic properties of the original recording media are known. But filtering aimed at minimizing at any cost surface noise, and crackle, is not to be tolerated.

' Of course occasional clicks can be excised from master plates, or cut out of tapes. And even, in exceptional circumstances, a torrent of crackle can be eliminated by carefully going over a tape transfer with tiny gobs of silencing material. But as can be imagined, for an LP side this runs into hundreds of hours of painstaking work. An instance of it being done, I believe, was by EMI in order to produce COLH142, Elena Gerhardt's volume for the Hugo Wolf Society. The masters no longer existed, and all that was available were sets of the shellac discs that moisture, fungi, and oxygen had had their innings at.

' That's the rub in this matter of *crackle*. On the one hand there are the big companies who *may* have masters for the original 78s. But usually only a limited amount of work can be devoted to these old recordings if the companies are to get a financial return on the LP transfer. And moreover, the big companies are tempted and frequently yield to over-filtering in order to reach the widest possible markets. On the other hand there are the collectors and institutions who might be interested in making documentary transfers (copyright restrictions aside). They are faced with the strong likelihood that copies of 78s they take off their shelves for this purpose will turn out to be riddled with *crackle*. And they, least of all, may be able to afford the time, or have the equipment, to do what EMI did for Elena Gerhardt.

' What is more, the big companies do not by any means have masters for all their 78s. For instance, RCA Victor in America seems to hold still a fairly high percentage of its red seal material from over the years, but to be very spotty otherwise. Columbia (CBS) has a lot of masters from the mid-'30s on, only odds and ends before that. As for EMI and the European situation, virtually all the pre-electric Odeon and Fonotipia material perished during the second world war. (As also did most of the older Gramophone Co masters held by DGG in Hanover.) In Britain the Gramophone Co's policy over the years was, evidently, to render down for re-use very shortly after withdrawal from the catalogue, practically any master not considered to be by a celebrity artist. In practice this meant most recordings in the plum and lower grade series. Also, as is fairly well known, EMI at Hayes does not hold masters for much Gramophone Co material dating prior to the transfer of plates from Hanover around 1910. Exceptions are recordings that were still in the English catalogue at that time, and the recordings of a few super-celebrities such as Tamagno, Caruso, Patti, and Melba that were regarded as akin to the crown jewels. On the basis of various evidence it can be estimated that of Gramophone Co masters by artists who would now be regarded as celebrities (regardless of their original label status) and recorded up to the beginning of the second world war, only about two-fifths, at the outside, still survive at Hayes. (At one time a good many masters for post-1910 ethnic recordings were extant there, but I have no idea whether this is still so.) As for Columbia and Parlophone masters, it seems that practically nothing exists beyond what was listed at the end of the second world war.'

This raises the general question of quality, as far as the original pressings are concerned. The American Columbia records had very bad surfaces, the Victor Red Seal (pre-second world war) very good ones. Certainly, different companies had good and bad periods, and in the UK, Columbia/HMV deteriorated after the early 1930s. Some recordings, such as the Moeran G minor symphony, which one would expect to be good, are all but ruined by the surfaces. But just at the very end of the 78 era Cetra evidently adopted a new formulation. Some of the pressings with red-white-and-brown labels are not only virtually crackle-free, but have extraordinarily quiet surfaces.

DIRECTLY RECORDED DISCS

Acetate discs, consisting of a recording medium on an aluminium or glass base, are known to have a limited life, although Pickett and Lemcoe's estimates[14] of eighteen to twenty five years have been exceeded by examples known to the present author. However it is clear it *has* a very limited life, and that the breakdown can happen without warning. Storage conditions are clearly critical.

The main disadvantage of such recording media is their softness, and hence their susceptibility to wear. To the discographer dealing with material owned by the composer himself such considerations are often critical. The experience of the present writer has been that composers have had broadcasts and public performances recorded for their own private use since at least the early 1930s, and a large number of these have remained in the composer's or his relatives' hands. However, the fact of the impermanence of the recording medium is usually not realised, and the recordings have often deteriorated, particularly after having been intensively played—usually on inferior equipment.

The following are the lessons to be learnt from such circumstances:

1 Always make approaches to the composer, or his family if he is deceased. My experience is that a friendly and helpful reception is to be expected in the majority of such cases.

2 After having obtained copyright clearance, have whatever is available copied as soon as possible, to ensure preservation. Make sure all documentation and details of the performers is obtained from the owner.

3 If the recording is recent, check back to see if the engineer or recording firm preserved a master-tape and approach them if possible.

4 Ask permissions as far as possible and treat the performing rights laws with circumspection. But ensure preservation before arguing—clearly a tight-rope has to be walked sometimes.

5 Preserve the original in case it is possible to make a better copy later.

TAPE

Experimentation with modern tapes has given rise to little published research. There has been no evidence demonstrating a lasting quality in modern polyester or PVC tapes. Even worse is the question of cassettes using very narrow tape. Although physically protected, they are very prone to physical damage to the actual tape. The fact that tape recorder and recording tape failure has been a major cause of breakdown in the US space programme, suggests that developments in this field may be expected soon (see *Report of the Tape Recorder Action Plan Committee*, March 21 1972, NASA, 1972).

A preoccupation of the early 1970s has been the reduction of all forms of mechanical noise in recordings. In particular, with the development of 'Dolby' noise reducing equipment, tapes are increasingly extant that have been 'doctored' in various ways and require special play-back equipment. The statement of these electronic links vital to the authentic recreation of the sound thus encoded must be recognised and noted by the discographer and cataloguer. Those most frequently met at the time of writing are 'Dolbyised' recordings—recordings made on machines which enhance a particular frequency range and correct on play-back, thus attenuating tape noise, and the

22

use of chromium dioxide tape on cassette recorders. The latter, under the trade name ' Crolyn ', is also made in reel-to-reel form for computer use, but has not found wide use for domestic audio equipment at the time of writing.

EARLY RECORDINGS

In the context of preservation, there is another aspect of some importance as far as the discography is concerned. This concerns recordings produced in the very early years of the century, and even in the late 1890s. Clearly, if recordings can be identified as having been made, from old catalogues and the remaining documentation of record companies or recording artists, then there is something to aim at. Such research is not as easy as it sounds, for although a few early catalogues have been reprinted in facsimile, many are difficult, if not impossible to find. So a comprehensive bibliography of early catalogues would be but a step to preserving a complete list of all historically important recordings. The problem is particularly acute when considering Russian and Central European material, where many gaps in our knowledge are still to be filled. Thus a discography locating examples of such early recordings, and indicating which have been re-issued in LP dubs (with notes as to technical quality) would be a welcome addition to Bauer (see page 94-95). *Not in Bauer* is a familiar comment in discographies, although not necessarily indicating a valuable or scarce record, which the statement always seems to imply.

LP REISSUES OF 78S

A wealth of material that was originally available on 78s (and indeed on film soundtrack) has been reprocessed and issued on LP—often several times in varied couplings. In the UK, copyright subsists in a recording for fifty years. Because of this fact there are a number of sources for 78 reissues :

1 Reissued by or by permission of original manufacturer.

2 Original masters repressed.

3 Out of copyright and reissued by company other than originally, often small independent company, or even private individuals.

4 Material not out-of-copyright, and pirated, usually by overseas companies.

The outcome of these factors is that the quality of such reissues is variable. It is imperative that any discographical citation of reissues should identify the origin of the recording, should ascertain that the dub has been made at the correct pitch, and that the artists and the material performed have been correctly identified. It is also of historical value to be able to date any record. Material in categories 1 and 2 above will almost certainly be more reliable than those in 3 and 4, although the latter may be of greater interest. A comprehensive catalogue of such records is an urgent necessity.

EMI started the practice of reissuing outstanding material dubbed onto LP in the 1950s, with its *Great recordings of the century* series. Since then, particularly under the pressure of dubbings made by other companies, they have both increased the range of material available and lowered their prices. Indeed, as an example of how a scholarly enterprise of great historical worth and artistic value should be carried out, the student should note the album entitled 'Images of Elgar' that HMV issued in 1972. In particular, the booklet accompanying the records is a model of its kind.

When a big company reissues material preserved in its own archives, and the transfers are made by an engineer of skill and experience, the results can often be better than the originals, and the surface noise almost certainly will be less. However, one should be aware of the various techniques that are employed to make an old recording sound more acceptable. From an archival and historical viewpoint it is best that the recordings should be dubbed without the upper frequencies being attenuated by filters, nor the middle frequencies being boosted to improve the sound of a soloist or singer. The whole point of the craft of dubbing is to transmit the *actual sound* of an historical event as authentically as possible. The unrestrained alteration of the 'sound' can only put the authenticity of the material in doubt, and should be noted by the discographer. Perhaps the supreme example of this is the re-recorded accompaniment to Kathleen Ferrier that Decca perpetrated in 1960 on SXL2234. (See *The gramophone* October 1960, p 208.)

The development of stereophony and quadraphony makes the task even more difficult. The discographer should always comment if he has personal and objective doubts about the authenticity of a recording.

The problem of technical quality is acute as far as some early pirate recording devices are concerned, and dubbing should be made from the original or a compatible machine. A note should be kept of the source of any recording and its method of transmission.

III

THE MEANING OF DISCOGRAPHY

The term 'discography' originated in the 1930s to describe a catalogue of sound recordings. At that time the only medium used for making such recordings was the disc; cylinder records were out-moded and no longer manufactured, and tape and other forms of recording had not been brought to practical realisation. Thus the fact that the physical format of a disc became synonymous with sound recordings made logical a term such as 'discography' to describe a catalogue of recordings on disc, and by extension any catalogue of sound recordings and associated material.

ORIGIN OF THE TERM

The earliest published use of the word discography appears to be in *Melody maker* in December 1935. However, it may well be that the term was in use verbally before it appeared in print. The first use of 'discography' in a scholarly tool is probably Charles Delaunay's *Hot discographie*, first published in France in 1936. While the impetus of amateur discographers in the jazz field pioneered the art of discography—as indeed they had to do in a field where the tradition was predominantly an aural one—the influence of *Darrell* was probably more considerable in the long run. It was the establishment of Darrell's encyclopedia in America in the 1930s, and *World encyclopedia of recorded music* in the UK in 1952, that gave the seal of respectability to what had been previously regarded as an amateur art. At the same time these two ventures provided the basic working tools for all future workers in this field.

Clough and Cuming wrote in their introduction that 'The principles and procedures of discography were laid down by R D Darrell in his *Gramophone Shop encyclopedia of recorded music* . . . and have been followed by subsequent compilers; the present work is planned on similar lines, and we must acknowledge what is indeed obvious, the inspiration and instruction we have derived from Darrell's work.'

Discography has developed as a concomitant of the activities of private collectors of gramophone records. Institutional libraries have, until recently, all but ignored recordings, unless the nature of the parent body (*eg* broadcasting stations) made them a necessary activity. As a result, accepted codes for cataloguing have only recently been widely promulgated. Thus the amateurs have created all the precedents from practical necessity in their individual speciality.

In the more general field, discography has also developed—and for the greater period of time—as the catalogues of the various record selling companies and shops have grown. The second-hand market has also been involved in this, and general standards for abbreviated, but classified (either by composer or performer) methods of listing have become accepted.

The comparison with bibliography is obvious. The same terminology can be used:

Historical discography—the history of the medium and its dissemination.

Analytical discography—all the matters that relate to the correct and authentic reproduction of the sound of a known event. This includes, on the technical side, questions of the speed at which the disc or tape should move (*ie* the correct pitch is reproduced) and obtaining the best possible sound from a given source. A number of American institutions, in particular, are giving close attention to such problems. On the other hand analytical discography can relate to questions of identification of particular works performed, or the editions or forms of such works, and also to questions of performing practice.

Systematic discography—the systematic listing of what has actually been recorded. Formerly this will have been necessarily restricted to commercial issues, but the major expansions in technology during the last ten years or so make it desirable that attempts should be made at including all sources. There are many possible arrangements for a systematic discography and these are discussed in chapter VIII.

Descriptive discography—in cataloguing *individual copies* of discs the presupposition must be made that having to describe the recording physically is necessitated by the rarity of the item concerned. The necessity for descriptive discography is therefore brought about either by the need to locate copies of rare items for reference purposes, or for description in sale catalogues.

Most dealers' second-hand catalogues have utilised a system of grading and description of the discs on offer. Three possible systems are shown here, all of which have been used successfully.

A fairly long established code of condition markings and abbreviations is that used by the 78 Record Exchange:

CODE OF CONDITION

FN	A perfect, unworn copy	Jt	Just touching
VVG-FN	Very slight signs of use, plays perfectly	LC	Lamination crack
		NA	Non-affecting
VVG	Wear more pronounced, plays well	NBA	Not broken away
		ND	Needle-dig
VG	Well worn but can still provide enjoyment	NR	Needle-run
		RC	Rim chip
G	Very worn—not quite useless	RS	Rough start
		Aff	Affecting
LSM	Light surface marks, rubs	Ext	Extending
		Int	Internal
PRF	Pressing fault, flaw	Num	Numerous
SCR	Scratch, scratches	Slt	Slight
ULC	Under-label crack	Lt	Light
BL	Blister	sd	Side
EB	Edge-bite	V	Very
GD	Groove-dig	w	With
HC	Hair-crack		

More recently, a simplified system of grading has been introduced in *Antique records*:

GRADING OF RECORDS

'We have tried to make our system of grading as simple as possible. We considered, very seriously, whether to change from the procedure which is generally in operation, but we decided finally to do so— simply because there seem to be so many different interpretations applied to that procedure.

'We have instituted four grades. These apply to all makes, regardless of age.

Immaculate	(Imm)
First class	(1st)
'Second'	(2nd)
Third rate	(3rd)

Immaculate—We do not believe that there is such a thing as a 'mint' record, since we feel certain that someone, somewhere must have played it. We regard an immaculate copy as one which is remarkably unused. There should be no marks or signs of wear of any

27

significance. Its appearance should be much the same as when it was first purchased from the retailer.

First class—This is the equivalent of the generally used term ' fine '. We consider a first class copy to be one which is almost visually perfect. There may well be some marks—but these should cause very little aural distraction.

' *Second* '—We have deliberately chosen this term, because a ' second ' is generally accepted as being a less than perfect article. A second would, we think, correspond to a ' VG ' copy. We believe, however, that this term is a misnomer—since such a copy is clearly not ' very good '. A ' second ' is a copy which has suffered some damage or wear. The marks and scores will be noticeable both aurally and visually. Generally speaking, however, it is quite a presentable and playable copy.

Third rate—This is all that the term implies. It cannot be described as good. It is battle-scarred and rather weary. It is, nonetheless, playable—but it may require patience to get the best from it.'

However, although not so easy to use, the system devised by John R T Davies and used in the short lived magazine *78 RPM* is probably the most exact, and is quoted in full because of its valuable and closely reasoned introduction:

THE CODING SYSTEM

'At present the disparity of grading among collectors is so great that it is no longer possible to buy a record unseen and unheard with any certainty of satisfaction.

' Some collectors grade their discs visually; some aurally. Since sound is the primary consideration, aural methods would appear superficially to be the best choice. However, such methods will, on examination, prove to be the least exact, due not only to variation in quality of recording and pressing, but also to a similar variety of methods of playback. We should remember that different companies used different varieties and qualities of shellac, which resulted, among other things, in a different basic level of surface noise. Also, many early records have a groove width which makes them impossible to reproduce electrically using a standard 78 stylus. The sound of a record does not, therefore, tell enough of its condition, and what it does tell may be very far from fact.

' *Wear and damage*—The present system of assessing the condition of a gramophone record allows for only a general overall condition rating, whereas there are, in fact, two distinct and separate factors with bearing on the acceptability of a record to its prospective purchaser: these are *wear*, brought about by the needle in the groove, and *damage*, brought about by other means.

' *Wear*—While the surface of a record may be dulled by general and uniform scuffing, or look dull as a result of poor material used for pressing, or other untoward factors in its manufacture, and on casual inspection appear to be worn generally, this may not be the case. The reverse may not be true either, boot-blacking having been used by some unscrupulous characters in the past. The *Buchmann-Meyer* effect is one manifestation virtually unaffected by these variables. This is the Christmas-tree like reflection seen in the grooved part of a gramophone record, and best seen from a $45°$ angle across the diameter of the record with a small but bright source of light on the same side as the viewer. In the case of a new, unplayed record this reflection is always bright and well-defined, with the individual contours of the modulated groove showing varying degrees of reflection so that the surface will appear to glitter. Lower notes will show quite distinctly as a series of dark and light flashes, higher notes as a series of light or dark dots or points; the higher the notes the smaller the points. What Buchmann and Meyer discovered was that the spread of the branches was directly proportional to the level of modulation in the groove. The reflection could be defined as " crisp, with well-defined limits ".

'As a record becomes worn the reflection becomes dull and the limits ill-defined. The glitter disappears—at first leaving a bright, non-glittering reflection, and then the brightness fades, and the reflection fades and the reflection becomes undefined, dull and lifeless—as does the music. As wear takes place and the glitter disappears the width of the reflection increases.

' *Damage*—Damage to a gramophone record may take many forms, but must be treated as a separate phenomenon from wear. Two main forms of damage can be defined.

General damage and particular damage

' General damage takes the form of scuffing, scratching and gritting. Scuffing is a name given to a relatively broad swath of extremely light parallel scratches. Scratches may be caused by any hard, sharp object drawn across the surface of a record, or vice-versa. The resulting furrow on the surface of the record may be light, cutting to only a tenth of the groove depth, where it will not normally be audible, or fairly heavy, cutting to half the depth of the groove. A scratch cutting to the bottom of the groove or deeper may well be termed a score.

'Gritting is a similar phenomenon to scratching, except that the hard, sharp object is usually between the record and something else (possibly another record in a pile) and does the damage either by being pressed into, or rolled across, the surface, chipping out various sized pieces of the record material, often in an otherwise than straight or curved line of non-continuous nature. Occasionally such an object will become embedded in the material of the record. As a rule, gritting leaves chips and pits in the groove wall sufficiently far down to be audible, sometimes leaving a hole similar to a small needle dig.

'General wear and damage form the basis for the following method of condition assessment.

The assessment and designation of the condition of gramophone records—At present a series of symbols is in use to show the condition of a record, up to two being used at any time. With no greater number of symbols, the two factors determining the general condition of a record can be accurately assessed. A table of assessments is shown below, based on a pair of scales which would show an absolutely mint record at 99 and a piece of useless shellac at 00. (NB: While a visual assessment will be more accurate in relatively unworn records and those showing definable wear and damage, aural assessment may prove practicable in the last stages of deterioration.) While the sum of the digits might reasonably be expected to indicate general condition, a record graded 56 might be of more value to a collector possessing good filtering equipment than one graded 74, which would be better used by a collector who has either a range of different playing styli or uses metallic needles. 38, on the other hand, might suit a collector who doesn't mind a general fall in quality, but cannot abide clicks and pops.

'The system might appear at first glance somewhat cumbersome, but in practice it is easy to use and does give a remarkably accurate " sight " of a record.' JRTD.

THE ASSESSMENT AND DESIGNATION OF THE CONDITION OF
GRAMOPHONE RECORDS
Wear
9 : Unplayed, and therefore unworn. (There can be few vintage 78rpm pressings still in this condition.)

8: Played. No visible wear even under a powerful magnifying glass. Marks around the centre will usually confirm use.

7: Lines of grey appear on loud peaks only.

6: Lines of grey on all loud passages and usually showing 'dashes' of grey in heavy bass passages.

5: Grey in all 'orchestra' or 'ensemble' passages. Only soft passages (such as piano soli) still bright and glittering.

4: Grey all over except silent and near silent passages. Groove wall damage readily visible in bass passages.

3: Grey all over. Groove wall damage visible in all except soft passages. Buchmann-Meyer effect noticeably dulled.

2: Really worn all over, bottom of the groove usually visibly worn. B-M effect definitely ill-defined.

1: Sound only just recognisable. Bottom of the groove often really well ploughed up.

0: Sound barely audible. Worn 'smooth'. B-M effect ceases to show except as general dully reflecting surface.

Damage

9: Undamaged in any way. Perfect in every way as it left the press; not even showing slight scuffs or incidental marking caused by handling at factory or shop.

8: Showing slight scuffs or incidental marking as caused by handling at factory or shop.

7: Heavy scuffing or marking. May show one or two light but distinct scratches.

6: Heavy scuffing and marking with light scratches and/or grit marks.

5: Heavy scuffing and marking with general scratching and gritting.

4: Heavy scratching and gritting; scuffing and marking become less discernible as they blend into the general condition.

3: As 4 but over most of the playing area scratching and gritting does not admit spaces of more than $\frac{1}{2}$in diameter.

2: Very heavy scratching and gritting and some scoring; over most of the playing area scratching, gritting and scoring does not admit spaces of more than $\frac{1}{4}$in diameter.

1: As 2 but including some very heavy scoring to bottom of groove and below. Listening difficult.

0: Listening is just not worthwhile.'

SCOPE OF DISCOGRAPHY

Today discography has developed to mean something much more exact than it meant in the 1930s. The term has become all-embracing.

Not only are commercially issued records included, but it has expanded to include all possible sources of sound recordings. The system has grown away from its origins and taken on a new and larger meaning. However, it is a convenient term, less cumbersome than others that have been suggested, and it will probably continue in use. Its actual scope today will include:

Discs

1 Coarse-grooved (at a variety of speeds between 78 and 90 rpm and between 7 and 16 inches in diameter, but more usually 78 rpm and 10 or 12 inches in diameter). These will include both laterally and vertically ('hill and dale') cut discs, starting at either the edge or the centre. The norm is taken to be edge-starting 78rpm discs, laterally cut, and 10 or 12 inches in diameter. All variations from this standard must be noted in any discographical entry. (In the case of recordings originating from wax masters, the metalwork is of particular importance in the long term preservation of the item concerned.)

2 Microgroove (usually at 45 or 33⅓ rpm, but other speeds are known, in diameters of 7, 8, 10 and 12 inches). These may be monophonic (*ie* one channel per groove), stereophonic (*ie* two channels per groove), or quadraphonic (*ie* four channels per groove).

Tapes

1 Reel to reel (usually at 3¾, 7½ or 15 inches per second, full, twin or quarter track); these may be either monophonic, stereophonic, or quadraphonic.

2 Cassette (always at the same speed—1⅞ inches per second—so no speed indication is necessary); these may be either monophonic, stereophonic or quadraphonic.

3 Cartridges; similar to cassettes, except they can accept up to eight tracks of recordings.

Other media

Usually only appropriate when a very full listing is made, including archive material, when direct-cut acetate non-commercial discs may be included, as well as film soundtracks and surviving older forms of custom-recording (wire recorders, steel-tape recorders, and the Philips and Miller non-photographic film recording system).

It should be noted that coarse-grooved records, while normally pressed in shellac, were sometimes pressed in vinyl in the 1940s and 1950s. Such a pressing should be shown.

IV

PRACTICAL DISCOGRAPHY

There are two clear stages in the compilation of any discography. Firstly, the conceptualisation of the actual subject matter, and the decision as to the scope of the work in hand (which may well develop as the work progresses). Secondly, the process of amassing the necessary information to be included, where to obtain the information, and its assembly.

DEFINITION OF THE SCOPE
Gordon Stevenson has produced a list of sixteen different systems (*Library trends* July 1972 p 118) by which discographies may be organised:

1 alphabetical based on composer's names
2 alphabetical based on titles of works recorded
3 by country or place of origin (where manufactured)
4 by country of origin (*eg* French music)
5 numerical, based on matrix numbers
6 numerical, based on catalogue numbers
7 chronological, by date of publication
8 chronological, by date of recording
9 chronological, by date of composition
10 arrangement based on some qualitative standard comparable to the 'best book' type of bibliography
11 alphabetical, based on names of performers
12 physical format
13 by subject or form (*eg* symphony)
14 the performing media (*eg* flute music)
15 status in the trade (*eg* out of print recordings)
16 arrangement (based on author's of text (*eg* settings of Shakespeare)

The nature of and need for a given compilation will usually have been the starting point for that compilation, so that the initial decisions tend to predetermine the nature of the work to be done. While Stevenson's list is a valid guide to thought, it is to some extent confusing. If, for example, one has to produce a bibliography as a trade guide to the commercial recordings in print in, say, Sweden, or as a guide to available recordings in a book on Schutz, or to demonstrate development of orchestral style between the wars, it is evident the division is more simply stated. Is it a *general* discography? Or is it a *subject* discography? Five clear categories emerge:

GENERAL

COMPOSER (the originator of the material recorded)

ARTIST (the re-creator of the material recorded)

SUBJECT (particularly in the case of non-musical recordings)

LABEL/NUMBERS (arranged from the manufacturing viewpoint, or in the case of archive recordings, the institution or point of origin).

At this point in the planning of a discography, the compiler has to limit his field. Is it to be *comprehensive*, covering all possible presentations of the subject matter, that is every surviving recording? Or is it to be limited by considerations of:

PHYSICAL FORMAT (LP discs, stereo cassettes, 78s etc)

COUNTRY OF ORIGIN

CHRONOLOGY (*eg* records issued since 1950)

CURRENCY (availability from the manufacturer)

AVAILABILITY (commercially issued recordings as compared with privately made or archive recordings).

These qualifying factors are not mutually exclusive, and may all apply.

It is worth noting that questions of chronology are often determined by technical factors (*eg* development of electrical recording in 1924/5), rather than artistic ones—the latter tending to apply only when questions of style of performance are of interest.

In the case of the discography being the catalogue of a specific archive, there will, of course, appear an incomplete listing of the commercial material theoretically available, as well as certain materials unique to that establishment.

The discographer should have clear in his mind whether it is his objective to establish the existence of the material under discussion, or merely to act as a guide to sources of illustrations relevant to a particular study. This is a question of either the particular *piece of sound* as an historical entity in itself, or a convenient aural representation of *a kind of sound*.

COMPREHENSIVENESS

A comprehensive listing of all sound recordings ever made is almost as impracticable as the nineteenth century aspiration to own all the books ever published. Nevertheless, within certain broad fields, approaches towards comprehensiveness have been made. The most notable of these is, of course, WERM. The aims of the compilers were set out in their introduction:

'We have aimed at the inclusion of every record of permanent music issued since the advent of electrical recording up to April, 1950, throughout the world . . . In addition, a few pre-electric records are included, either because the music has not been recorded again or because of the interest of the performance. . .'

The comprehensiveness of that volume is in many places in doubt, but often this must be ascribed to its compilers' decision as to what is and what is not of ' permanent ' value.

The concept of comprehensiveness as far as composer discographies are concerned has only recently been developed to the full, in, for example, Westerlund and Hughes *Monteverdi discography* (BIRS, 1970), or Clough and Cuming's *List of recordings* (in Kennedy's *The works of Ralph Vaughan Williams*, OUP, 1964, p 725-746), supplemented by their *Discography 1964-1971* (in *The music yearbook 1972-3* Macmillan, 1972, p 150-160). A host of comprehensive discographies have appeared in *Recorded sound*.

My own discography of Sir Arnold Bax (*Recorded sound* January/April 1968, p 277-283) aimed at comprehensiveness, and a list of the subheadings used shows the range of material that may be aimed at in such works:

1 Recordings of works by Bax in chronological order of composition. (An entry is made for every piece of music by Bax that has been recorded, although when it comes into one of the categories below, it is merely indicated by a cross-reference.)

2 Commercially issued tapes.

3 Projected and forthcoming commercial records.

4 Recordings in the BBC Sound Archives.

5 Non-commercial recordings in the British Institute of Recorded Sound.

6 Non-commercial recordings in the Library of Congress.

7 Films with music by Bax.

8 Recordings of Bax's voice.

9 Piano rolls.

10 Bax as a performer: (i) in his own music; (ii) in other's music.

11 Broadcasts by or on Bax of which scripts are preserved.

12 Alphabetical list of recorded works.

35

The requirements of work on this scale are: to realise the range of material that is potentially available; and to make sure the compilation is adequately indexed—a classified arrangement is of restricted value if there is no easy means of access to it. In more recent composer-discographies in *Recorded sound,* attempts have been made to produce such compilations in one self-indexing alphabetical sequence. Certainly this makes for compactness, but at the expense of the ability to approach material by format or location—not a problem in a small study, but a crippling one in a large work.

Artist-discographies have been most extensively developed in the field of vocal recordings. Simple artist-discographies have probably been appearing for longest of all, certainly as long as popular figures have been written up in the music and record press on the basis of their recordings. In such cases it has been the practice for a list of recordings to be appended, although in the early days the actual record numbers were often not given.

However, in the matter of performance, we find one of discography's most important contributions to scholarship. For in the examination of the actual sounds of the performances of the past, we find ourselves in a situation impossible before the technological breakthrough represented by recording techniques. The facility of being able to juxtapose the actual sound of different aural traditions will become more important as the period of availability of this facility lengthens. The discography is the tool by which these materials may be brought together. Thus the discographer should always bear in mind that he is enabling the performers and performing traditions of the past to be assessed by standards of a different period: a viable comparative criticism is being made possible based on the actual performances of different periods of history.

As recording is such a recently developed science, the discographer's responsibility is an important one: that of ensuring that the materials of the past as we have them in recorded form are transmitted correctly. Not only in technical terms (that the records are reproduced correctly, at the correct speed) but also in artistic terms. What, for example, were the circumstances under which a particular recording was made? Can it be regarded as an authentic representation of the artists concerned? Such matters should be viewed in the light of contemporary printed documentation. What *were* the reasons for a given performer's admiration by his fellows? Such matters might well be of great relevance to the discographer, in deciding the importance of a given recording, and might well influence the physical layout of his work. Discography only *begins* with the mechanical collection of the details of what does and does not exist.

WORKING METHODS

The practical methods for the physical collection of the entries for a particular discography are largely a matter of temperament. Eventually it will be desirable to have them all accurately written (or typed) on cards or slips, thus facilitating changes in arrangement, and also allowing for the insertion of new entries in the sequence.

It might appear somewhat obvious, but nevertheless worth stating, that if the entries are accurately made, at this stage, and consistent in their form of entry, they may be used to provide the final copy for the typist or typesetter, and thus save a lot of laborious transcription.

However, the use of a note-book is favoured by some, and while this means at the very least that the entries have to be copied out or photocopied, it also means that a chronological record of compilation is kept which may well be of value in those indefinable matters of association and intuition that differentiate the outstanding compilation from the merely conscientious. In such matters it is largely a question of habit—one uses the medium with which one feels the most at ease.

If it is desired to make the file analysable by a variety of parameters —conductor, orchestra, soloists, record label, even writers of sleeve notes—then edge-punched cards are the most practicable method.[53] This technique allows one to punch out holes for various factors using gridded cards. Later all the cards representing a particular feature may be revealed by inserting a rod which holds together the remainder of the pack while the others are removed.

SEARCHING

When starting work on any discographical project, a number of questions have to be decided upon at the outset. Among these will be matters of layout and arrangement, which are discussed in the following chapters.

However, in the practical assembly of the information to be included, the actual choice of sources and method of working will have implications for the final scope and authenticity of the compilation in question. Thus the sources of the information—from sound libraries, catalogues, from other discographies, or from the records themselves—are of importance. The nature of the sources will give rise to further problems of authentication and identification of the materials concerned, and may necessitate comparative hearings to decide upon the way in which the technical quality of the recordings affects the transmission of the music or other sound-record thereby presented.

BIBLIOGRAPHIES
Before embarking on any major piece of work it is essential to check that one is not repeating someone else's efforts. Unfortunately there is no equivalent of Bestermann's celebrated bibliography of bibliographies in the discographical field. The BIRS published a short bibliography in *Recorded sound* (Summer 1962, p 206-213), which was mainly artist-orientated, but also included short lists headed : ' General ', ' Vertical cut ', ' Makes of records ', ' Types of material ', and individual composers. Since then the present author has produced a supplementary bibliography (*Discographies: a bibliography*, Triad Press, 1973). However, there is clearly a need for a *major* bibliography of discographies. The BIRS discography covered the journal literature for the period up to 1962 for ' serious ' music.

Since then, *Recorded sound* has published an invaluable cumulated index (October 1971, p 805-827) which indexes the *Bulletin of the BIRS* and *Recorded sound* in one sequence, and is in fact a major guide to the discographical work of the 1960s. Other journals should be checked from their annual indexes (*eg The gramophone* and *The record collector*). In this respect a search in the *Music index* and *Rilm abstracts* will often be profitable. The major problem in this sort of area is the ' little magazine '—*78 RPM, Record advertiser, Antique records*. They are not indexed and may be little known. Particularly when they have ceased publication they can be very difficult to find. Often it will be a case of word of mouth, and one may have to resort to personal contacts—the writers of columns about record collecting in the press, the staff of record libraries and archives, even the BBC. However, one should not use such sources lightly, although the present writer has always found the experts to be unwaveringly friendly, and indeed has always been pleased to give advice in his own specific field.

Possibly the most difficult source to trace is the discography included in a monograph on the subject of the proposed discography. Such sources are usually highly selective, and Malcolm Walker's *Barbirolli discography* (*In* Michael Kennedy's *Barbirolli*, MacGibbon

& Kee 1971, p 338-402), Ivan Lund's *Stokowski* (*In* Edward Johnson's *Stokowski*, Triad Press 1973, p 85-114), or Steven Smolian's *Fauré discography* (*In* Emile Vuillermoz' *Gabriel Fauré*, Philadelphia, Chilton Book Co 1969, p 173-259) are important exceptions in their fields and are indexed together with other similar studies in the author's *Discographies—a bibliography*. But far more difficult to trace, for example, would be 'Recordings made by Percy Grainger' (*In* T C Slattery's thesis, *The wind music of Percy Aldridge Grainger*, University of Iowa unpublished PhD, 1967).

GENERAL DISCOGRAPHIES

For some purposes the listings of currently available material in such publications as *The gramophone classical record catalogue*, or Schwann, may suffice and no actual work will be necessary. In any case the major general and commercial listings will almost always be the starting point.

Before starting a specific search it will usually be possible to gain some general idea of the scope of the project in hand by examining the entries in the major commercially published discographies. The major historical volumes are the basis (BAUER, WERM, DARRELL), and the current discographies continue them: *Gramophone LP catalogues*, *Schwann*, *Bielefelder*, and Santandrea's *Catalogo generale dischi microsoli*. It is necessary to build up good long files of these, or have access to a library holding them.

Thus one may quickly assemble into one sequence a rough starting point for future investigation. (It may be mentioned that errors occur in all these publications, and verification must be made where possible.)

There will almost certainly be discs that will have been found listed in discographies but copies of them remain untraced. Clearly they have to go in, but it might be wise to indicate that these entries are unheard.

SOURCES

Four sources may be regarded as primary for the purpose of the discography of published recordings.

1 The records themselves
2 Manufacturers' catalogues
3 Manufacturers' unpublished documentation
4 Manufacturers' advertisements.

A large personal or institutional collection in a given field can be a very useful starting point. Thus, starting from the recordings the discographer actually owns, the search can be extended to the holdings of large libraries and to other personal collections if the personal contacts exist. Often this sort of search may be accelerated by a classified advertisement in the record press. In particular, *The gramophone* and the *Record collector* reach the widest audience of enthusiasts, and are the most effective. *Opera* is also a useful medium when dealing with opera. Some specialist institutional collections may well have unique material, such as that of American music, which was formerly the loan collection of the USIS in London, and is now housed at Senate House (London University Library). A useful catalogue was issued (see figure II) while it was the USIS, and some unusual and unissued material may be found. The numerical catalogues of all manufacturers are particularly valuable tools, and increase in value as time passes. In this respect it is necessary to learn some of the history of various recording companies, when they flourished, and when they went out of business, and who took over the catalogues of companies no longer trading. There will be certain years when the catalogue will contain most of the particular company's issues in one sequence. By selecting catalogues spread at suitable intervals it is often possible to trace most of the issues of that company. Occasionally, reference to gramophone journals of the period concerned may show advertisements or reviews of items otherwise missed—in particular those in circulation for a short time, not included in WERM, or on a label whose catalogues are scarce (*eg* Waldo Warner, whose music was recorded on Vocalion). This becomes more valuable the further back one goes.

Naturally, if access is possible to archive material belonging to particular companies, so much the better. Compilations such as Moore's *Elgar discography* (BIRS, 1963) could not have been made so complete without such information—even though in this case it was based on an actual collection of discs.

MATRIX NUMBERS
When dealing with shellac discs, the importance of the matrix number is considerable, because it establishes the identity of any issue or re-issue incontrovertibly. Because the manufacturing process of a shellac disc commenced with the direct cutting of an impression into a wax master at the recording session, and because each disc thus cut was allotted a unique number which was likewise cut into the wax, in a strict numerical sequence, a unique method of dating and identification is available. Issued discs will have this number between the

end of the recorded face and the beginning of the label. From this it is possible to see which particular ' take ' was actually issued. Even more important, one can trace whether the actual recording of a side was changed, even though the number allotted to it in the manufacturer's catalogue was not. (One of the most important examples of this is the two versions of the scherzo of Vaughan Williams *Sixth symphony*. The 78rpm recording (LPO Boult) used the original version of the score when it was first issued (the scherzo is on c3875—2 sides). After Vaughan Williams revised the movement, it was re-recorded and reissued under the same number. However, by checking the matrix number, it is possible to identify the versions without playing the record. (The earlier version has matrix numbers 2EA 13627-1 and 13628-1).

This is also of interest where details of all the ' takes ' of a particular session are available, and also when sets of test pressings turn up which do not bear the same matrix numbers as the issued discs.

AUTHENTICATION AND IDENTIFICATION

Ideally, the only final and authoritative assessment that can be made of any item it is intended to include in a discography depends on listening to the recording, score or text in hand.

Naturally, the label and packaging is the first guide to the contents, and in the majority of cases this is authoritative. Nevertheless it should not be accepted unchecked. There may be sins of omission. Reviews or listings in extant discographies may provide a clue.

At this juncture a few examples might be in order, to give an idea of the sort of problems that arise. These are of particular importance in areas where minor alterations have been made in scores by living composers (*eg* Vaughan Williams), or where cuts are often made in long works (*eg* Rachmaninoff, Glière). At the beginning of the 78 era, works were frequently abridged to fit the restrictions imposed by a four-minute side. As far as acoustical recordings of orchestral music are concerned, textual authenticity was rarely possible. Alterations will often be found to have been made to facilitate the recording. Even today some conductors continually re-orchestrate works. (In Beethoven, conductors as different in style as Toscanini and Schmidt-Isserstedt add unauthentic orchestral timbres and doublings.)

The question of the repeat is one that tends to go by default. However, if a repeat is asked for in the score and is observed, the recording is obviously more authentic than one that omits the repeat in the cause of brevity. I would agree with Geoffrey Cuming when he writes[94]:

'Repeats? You may think this is the height of pedantry. Myself, I wouldn't advocate bothering about them as a general rule, but there are works where the observance of a repeat is a very important matter. The chief example is Mendelssohn's *Italian symphony*. Here we have a passage of 23 bars leading back to the repeat of the exposition, which is, I think one might say, usually ignored. Now if Mendelssohn had written the exposition out in full twice over instead of using a couple of convenient dots, no conductor on earth would have dared to omit the first time through and the bridge passage, and start where the exposition began for the second time; but because Mendelssohn uses this normal notation, they unblushingly cut a passage which is not heard later in the movement. So a conductor who does make the repeat deserves to have the fact mentioned on the card. Now you may think that by singling out a detail like this I'm bringing a value-judgment into what ought to be strictly objective and scientific work. Perhaps I am, but I can only say that in this job you need to have a passion for truth to carry you through at all, and I don't see why the occasional virtuous artist shouldn't have a pat on the back.'

Many problems arise in the dubbing of music from 78rpm discs to LP. When entering such transfers in the discography, it should be possible to indicate the source of the dubbed sound (*ie* record and matrix number), and whether it is a faithful transfer. Has the sound been tampered with and 'improved', or indeed really improved, as in the case of the EMI Elgar reissues? Most of the major British companies are scrupulous in this respect, but many of the smaller operators are not. *The gramophone*'s reviews of such reissues can be a convenient way of tracing the required information, as it is normally given in full. At this point it should be established that the item has, in fact, been dubbed at the correct speed, and again reviews are often a useful source if no copies of either the original or the music are available. (See Stratton's comments on the whole question of LP reissues of 78s quoted on pp 18-21).

Further similar questions of authenticating sources arise when dealing with 'pirate' recording. Particularly in the USA, many small companies are operating in which the issued recordings are 'pirated'. That is, they are issued from recordings made without the artists' permission, or payment being made. The sources of such materials are radio broadcasts, unauthorised recordings made at public performances, and from private archives of collectors often dating back to the 1930s. Dubbings of rare, commercially issued 78s also appear, although many of these are of material out of copyright. Clearly such recordings are often of outstanding artistic and historic interest. In such cases questions of authentication may be crucial and difficult. But they should always be treated with caution, and if necessary the item can be listed with ' unauthenticated information taken from label ', as a note of caution added by the discographer.

TRANSMISSION OF PRIVATELY HELD MATERIAL

The vast mass of recorded material (some dating from as far back as the early 1920s) that survives in private hands can pose considerable problems. Most of these recordings have been taken from broadcasts—firstly on 78rpm acetate discs, later on LP acetate discs, and later still on tape. A variety of strange media have ensured the preservation of valuable materials—wire recorders, Telefunken steel-tape recorders (note that the German experiments in early tape recording mean considerable archives are held by German radio stations), even dictaphones. Where a recording is of a public performance, or has been privately recorded for a special purpose, it is usually possible to authenticate it from documents originating from the same source as the recording—letters, handbills, programmes, receipts for disc cutting, maybe even personal reminiscences. However, if, for example, one is presented with a recording taken from the air, but not otherwise identified, special means have to be adopted for tracing it, and this can often be time consuming. Firstly, verbal inquiries should be made at the source of the recordings—if at a jumble sale, where did they come from? If from someone's lumber room, who made them? It should be remembered that acetate discs rarely last more then twenty five years and should be copied as quickly as possible *by someone who knows what he is doing;* similarly with early tape and wire recordings. It may be desirable to play the recording on its original machine for copying purposes. Remember also, once copied the original recording should be carefully stored—it might be possible to improve on it later.

It has been known for information given by amateur enthusiasts to be not only unreliable, but misleading. If one is dependent on a particular source to authenticate an otherwise unknown recording, a note of the source of information should always be made.

Two examples of the problems of authentication spring to mind. Firstly, the present writer had access to a privately made recording of Bantock's *Pagan symphony* made in 1936. It was not known from which broadcast the recording came, but it was thought to be by Henry Wood, though there was the possibility of it being a recording of a performance Beecham gave of the work at much the same time. Although I had noted the recording as 'performer unknown, slight possibility Beecham', it was listed by an enthusiast as an extant Beecham recording in a discography published in the USA.

Secondly, from the large catalogue of 'pirated' recordings of opera issued by various American labels, items have come to light of which the label is not an accurate description.

DATING OFF-THE-AIR DUBS

Occasionally the discographer will find that he has to deal with material recorded from the radio. Problems of identification may then arise. If a date and place of broadcasting can be established, it is possible then to trace the item in question through the *Radio times* (in the UK) or some similar publication elsewhere. Files of the *Radio times* may be searched at the Westminster Public Library, BBC, BIRS or the British Museum. It is worth remembering, also, that the circumstances of any broadcast should be noted in deciding whether the broadcast was a regional one (important during the 1930s and 1950s), or even local (important today).

In the United States, making disc recordings of broadcasts was something of a rich man's pastime in the 1930s, and a surprisingly large amount of material has survived—often with announcements, which allow for authentication of the performance details.

Another sort of disc which can often be of great historical importance is the radio transcription disc. Most European stations circulate transcription discs, which in theory are supposed to be defaced after a given time. However, in practice many are preserved. They command very high prices on the second-hand market, particularly in the USA (see page 18).

TECHNICAL QUALITY

If a discography is being based on a specific collection, or if it is of material existing in unique copies, a note of technical quality will often be of value. This is particularly relevant in the case of acetate discs, very old shellac records and cylinders.

All disc records are subject to wear. Before the advent of light-weight pick-ups, wear on 78s was considerable. Acetates wore even more quickly, particularly as the composers for whom such recordings were often made never appeared to realise the value of their own recordings.

Test pressings are often preserved as originators' copies—that is, the original sample discs supplied to the recording artists. It is possible to authenticate them from the matrix numbers. Indeed the only permanent storage medium that ensures fidelity is the metal master from which the discs were pressed. In this context the matrix number in any listing is all important. In Italy, for example, this is especially important, since the 'metal work' has been the archive storage medium for some time. It is interesting to remember that HMV deposited a number of metal masters with the British Museum between the wars, although they are now housed at the BIRS.

V

THE PRINCIPLE OF ENTRY SUBSTITUTION

When cataloguing a book, the entry is almost always derived from the title page, where there usually appears a formal title. Most bibliographic records are founded on a transcription of that title page. However, in the case of music, both recorded and printed, a problem arises, in that the work in question may be styled in many different ways. Thus:

Piano concerto no 5 in Eb, op 73, ' The Emperor '
Concerto for piano and orchestra, op 73
Eb Concerto
Op 73 Concerto
The Emperor concerto
Fifth concerto
Fifth piano concerto

and all
in many
different
languages

are all adequate and recognisable descriptions of the same work, that would suffice in conversation between musicians. However, in compiling a catalogue, such looseness of description can give rise to problems of alphabetisation and identification, cause double entries, and are generally confusing.

Therefore, before commencing compilation of a discography, a standard layout (or form of entry) should be decided upon and followed. The description of the work as it appears on the documentation with a recording (including announcements on ex-radio tapes) is therefore only to be taken as identification of the contents, and not the *way* in which the entry will be made. Such documentation in any case should always be regarded with a certain amount of suspicion.

If we consider the example already made,
Piano concerto no 5 in Eb op 73 ' The Emperor ',
it may be seen there are five elements:

The medium
The form
The key
The opus number and serial number (*ie* usually the chronology)
Popular title.

The form: In many cases this will be the most suitable to use as a filing term, thus bringing together, for example, all the solo instruments. In cases where works have been written for unorthodox combinations, this is almost always the best decision, thus:

Sonata for violin and cello, *not*
Violin and cello sonata.

The key: Other than for very special purposes, an arrangement by key is unlikely.

Opus or catalogue numbers: This is often a good way of entering works, and is useful if it is required to show chronology (although it should be remembered that such numbers may not always be chronologically accurate).

Popular title: An entry in which this element is the prime one of the entry, will be more appropriate to avant-garde composers, where the old formal titles are less frequently used, than in the context of a discography of a classical composer.

Sub-entries: The publication of excerpts from a larger work, often but not always operatic in nature, is a concept peculiar to recordings as a medium. In creating a substituted entry for such a document there are two considerations to be taken into account:

1 The entry for the overall work
2 The entries for the parts that work, arias, interludes, choruses etc, that constitute the recording under consideration.

Again the nature of the compilation in question will dictate the form of the entry, and in some cases, particularly artist-discographies, certain arias may be entered separately, for example:

Ich werde sie nicht wiedersehen
(Die Tote Stadt—Korngold)

or

DIE TOTE STADT: Ich werde sie
nicht wiedersehen (Korngold).

This gives rise to a further problem for which a substituted entry is necessary, namely that of vocal works performed in a variety of languages. We will return to this shortly.

There has been a number of solutions of the broader problem involving complex and confusing relisting of the separate excerpts of large works, but that developed by the *Gramophone classical record catalogue* is so simple and so effective, that it is the best model to follow in most general discographies. In such a listing, a formal entry is made for the work in question, and then a numerical list is made of the possible excerpts to be listed. The actual entries being made by the numbers thus allocated:

Rigoletto—Opera (1851-Veñice)
Cpte. 5s. nas. Serafin   (2/56) (R) MWS817
Cpte. 5s. nas. Molinari-Pradelli
                             (9/68) (R) SLS933
Cpte. 4s. nas. Molinari-Pradelli
                     (7/60) (5/68) (R) 6737 002
Cpte. 6s. Sanzogno   (6/62) SET224/6
Cpte. 4s. Solti   (1/65) SER5516-7
Cpte. 6s. nas. Kubelik   (1/65) (R) 270 9014
Cpte. 4s. nas. Perlea   (1/58) (R) VIC6401
(Excerpts.(ACT 1) 1a. Prelude: 1b. Delle mia bella
(Recit.); 2. Questa o quella (Ballata); 3. Partite?
Crudele?; 4. Gran nuova; 5. Ch'io gli parli; 6.
Quel vecchio maledivami (Duet); 7a. Pari siamo
7b Figlia! mio padre! (Duet); 7c. Ah! Deh non
parlare (Duet); 8a. Giovanna! ho dei rimorsi
(Recit.) 8b. T'amo, t'amo (Love Duet); 9a.
Gualtier! Malde (Recit.); 9b. Caro nome;
10a. Silenzio; 10b. Zitti zitti; (ACT 2) 11a. Ella
mi fu rapita (Recit.); 11b. Parmi veder la
lagrime (Aria); 11c. Scorrendo uniti remota
(Trio); 12a. Povero Rigoletto (Recit.); 12b.
Cortigiani (Aria); 13. Mio padre! Dio! (Recit.);
14a. Tutto le feste al tempio; 14b. Vendetta
tremenda (Finale); (ACT 3) 15a. E l'ami?
Sempre (Recit.); 15b. La donna a mobile (Can-
zone); 16a. Un di se ben (Quartet); 16b. Bella

figlia (Quartet); 17. M'odi; ritorna a casa
(Recit.); 18a. Ah! piu non ragiona (Trio); 18b.
Storm Music;19.Della vendetta (Recit.) 20a. Chi
e mai (Duet); 20b. V'ho ingannato (Duet).)

Excerpts from Recording on SET224-6:
2, 7, 9, 12, 14, 15b, 16, 20
                  (3/63) SXL6008, LXT6008
Excerpts from Recording on SAN204-6:
1, 2, 7, 8, 9, 10, 12, 14, 15b, 16b (10/70) ASD2595

Other Excerpts:
2, 6, 8, 9, 10b, 11c, 12, 14, 15b, 16b, 20. 2s.
Melis, Laszlo, Ilosfalvy, Body, Hungarian State
Opera, Gardelli   (6/69) SLPX11389
2, 16. Rec. J. BJORLING, R. Merrill, R. Peters,
A. Rota   (10/64) RB6585
2. Rec. Jussi BJORLING (r. 1944) (11/59) ALP1620
9. Rec. Joan SUTHERLAND (4/66)SXL6193
9. Rec. Anna MOFFO (6/61) (6/69) (R) SREG2064
9. Rec. Joan SUTHERLAND (12/60) SXL2257
9. Rec. Joan SUTHERLAND (4/66) SXL6190
12. Rec. D. FISCHER–DIESKAU   (1/69) 135008
15b. Rec. Jussi BJORLING (r. 1937)
                         (7/61) ALP1841
15b. Rec. Jozsef SIMANDY (2/71) SLPX11423
☐★15b. Rec. Placido DOMINGO (12/71) SER5613

There is no ' right ' way of compiling such an entry, which should be tailored to the job in hand, but having decided upon an order of elements, it is essential that this order is maintained within a given compilation. As in all bibliographic work, ' be consistent ' is the most important rule.

The medium: By bringing the medium to the fore in a work including a soloist, all the works for that particular instrument will fall together in the listing. Clearly a work formally known as ' double concerto ' will introduce additional problems. Such an entry could be made under ' Double ' if the composer had written a number of such works for different combinations, thus:

Double concerto for forte piano and harpsichord

Double concerto for two violins.

However, such listings can become increasingly unwieldy, and give rise to unidiomatic usage. Thus a concerto for orchestra, if entered under the medium, would produce a clumsy inversion:

Orchestra, concerto for.

The problem of language is a frequent one, and again is open to a solution that is more or less arbitrary. Compare:

Twilight of the Gods

Götterdämmerung

Le Crépuscule des Dieux.

The most practical solution is to list the material in the language in which it originated or is most commonly known. Any variations from this norm are listed in the same way, but an indication is made of the language of the performance.

Arrangements: The problem of substituted entries in the case of arrangements of parts of larger works is a particularly difficult question, made more so recently by the issue of short excerpts from larger works which have been used as theme music in television programmes and films. Thus a record of the ' Theme from the Onedin Line ' would in fact merit an entry as follows:

KHATCHATURIAN, Aram (b 1903)
 Spartacus—ballet: Adagio of Spartacus
  and Phrygia. [Used and recorded as
  signature tune to BBC Television series
  ' The Onedin Line '.]

The main problem in such a case will often be one of identification, and in the last resort an entry may have to be made with the note ' unidentified '. Otherwise a formal substituted entry should be made, with a brief annotation as to the circumstances of the recording.

SUMMARY

Thus we may summarise:

 1 Identify the music

 2 Decide on the elements to be used and their order (if necessary take a model as authority)

 3 Annotate any descriptive matter from label or sleeve, and index or cross-refer to this if necessary.

VI

LAYOUT

The formal bibliographic record for a book has developed over a considerable period of time. A great deal of scholarly attention has been paid to it, and highly sophisticated formats have been evolved. A parallel between the record made of a book and that of some other audio-visual medium is profitable, enabling one to make use of an established tradition while adapting it to suit new conditions and materials. The mistake that discographers and cataloguers of sound recordings have made in the past is to treat the new materials according to the techniques developed for print, without recognising the difference between what has gone before and what is requiring attention now.

Various degrees of fullness are possible in an entry for a book:

1 Full Standard Bibliographical Description (a very detailed description of a particular copy).

2 Standard Bibliographical Description (a general, but very detailed collation, including the contents).

3 Standard Catalogue Entry (a full listing of the book, giving author, title, publisher and collation).

4 Short Title Entry (usually just author, title, publisher and date).

A recording is only a source of information, as is a book, or printed music, and may, indeed, contain the same matter as a given book, but in an aural form. This may seem to be stating the obvious, but it is important to recognise that all that has changed is the medium through which the information is transmitted. It is this change in medium that is the essential difference between the two and dictates the necessity for a different approach. Thus, except when dealing with translations or classical works, the main entry of a published document with a formal title will be the title as it appears on the title page. The entry is thus a transcription of the title page, or is at least derived from it. However, in the case of sound recordings there will be no title page as such, and thus, the ' title ' must be a description of the material recorded. The sleeve and the label of a disc recording, while usually an invaluable guide to the contents, must only be regarded as a *guide* and not necessarily conclusive, accurate, or given with the title in the correct format. Normally, of course, for trade lists and abbreviated cataloguing of current commercial lists the label may be regarded as conclusive, and in the case of pop-music, it may be the only authoritative source. Nevertheless it is not always conclusive, and occasionally examples of mislabelling occur, although these are usually picked up in the reviewing press. Occasionally also, labels can be reversed. The only final assessment of the contents of any recording is to listen to it score or text in hand.

In this context it is interesting to consider two cases of mislabelling that I have experienced personally. In the first an early LP recording of the Glazounov *Sixth symphony* was issued with the first side containing the first movement cut onto the disc twice and the second movement omitted altogether (Kingsway 2911). In my second example a record labelled as containing Samuel Barber's *Cello sonata* actually contained Kodály's *Sonata op 4* (Stradivari STR 602). In the latter case, of course, not all examples of the record that are found exhibit the error.

ELEMENT IDENTIFICATION

In the chapter *User needs and bibliographic control of nonprint media* in the American Library Association's *Bibliographic control of nonprint media*[79], an attempt was made to establish which were the essential elements for bibliographic control of nonprint media, based on the requirements of the user. Fourteen elements were stated, of which seven have a specific importance in the context of a discography:

1 The title, which in the case of ' serious ' music will be a substituted and formalised one.

2 The creator will be the composer or composers (problems arise when dealing with pieces of music written by more than one composer, *eg* the Kutchka—the Five, Les Six or the FAE sonata by Brahms, Schumann and Dietrich), or in the case of improvised music the performer or group. (See also under 5 below.)

3 An edition statement will often have to be made in the light of technical innovation, and the re-processing of material (*eg* simulated stereo).

4 The recording date is the production date, and may be very different to the release or issue date. (Moore's *Elgar* is a good example of a discography arranged by recording date; Lund and Johnson's *Stokowski* an example of an arrangement by issue date.) Complications may occur when dealing with archival material unissued at the time

of its recording which is released later, if an arrangement by release date is adopted.

5 Producer. The concept of producer will not normally be of value, and yet may be appropriate in certain cases, particularly where a technique of presenting a recorded performance in a particular way has an influence on the concept of the music in question, and of more general questions of aesthetics: for example John Culshaw's recordings for Decca. Different recording engineers will use different techniques which might result in a similar performance *sounding* differently.

Transcripts made by different *engineers* can result in dubbings of different quality. Often the name of the engineer in question can be something of a guarantee of authenticity. As computer-techniques of eliminating background and surface noise improve, the question of the authenticity of the final product must be borne in mind. In this connection mention must be made of the exemplary quality of the transcriptions of 78s onto LP which Anthony Griffith has made for World Record Club and HMV.

6 Release date. The actual issue date will almost always be associated with the appearance of reviews, and may be of value for copyright purposes, and for discovering critical comment about a particular performance. In the case of the *Gramophone LP catalogue* it is important to realise that it is an index to reviews appearing in the *Gramophone* magazine.

7 Distributor. The issuing company, and hence the manufacturer's number is of unique importance in the field of sound recordings, where distribution arrangements are much quicker than in conventional publishing, and where they rely on the manufacturer's number. Expiry of contracts has meant the reappearance of the same material on a variety of differing labels, again important as a certain cutting, processing or pressing of a given performance may reproduce that performance more successfully than others.

(The interested reader may care to compare my list and analysis with that in the ALA's study—p 60.)

LIBRARY CATALOGUES AND DISCOGRAPHIES

A library catalogue can, of course, be a discography and a valuable one, but it will be limited by the holdings of the particular institution to which it refers. Of course it will also be enriched in the same way if that organisation holds particularly unique or rare material. The

BIRS were sufficiently cagey to describe their *Music by British composers of the twentieth century* (BIRS, 1967) as a ' Handlist of tape recordings in the Institute's collection '. Nevertheless it comes within the terms of reference of discography and demonstrates just such a point. It is a library catalogue and at the same time a valuable discography.

Usually a library catalogue will be on cards, and they may be part of a mixed-media collection, in which case although they could still be carrying out the functions of a discography, they could not be described as such. However, except when under compilation, discographies as such will rarely be on cards—the implication is of a printed or typescript catalogue. The major exception being the WERM entries after volume three, which are maintained at the BIRS on cards, although strangely enough the entries are not made one per card, but one card per work, often with many lines of entries.

REASONS FOR A RECORDING EXISTING

While deciding on the ways in which a discography or library catalogue entry may be made, in the music field, it is pertinent to consider the reasons for which music is recorded. J L Morgan in his supporting paper T for the *Study on the scope for automatic data processing in the British Library*[47] wrote:

' *Gramophone records*. Music on records often enough presents different characteristics from the printed score. It might well be thought that the scores/part division mentioned above with maximum and reduced detail printing would be equally reflected in recorded performance but this is only superficially so. Works are indeed performed complete or as excerpts but nearly always in maximum detail or arrangement terms; it would be difficult to recall recordings of a vocal score of an opera or of a piano concerto arranged for two pianos, and the Liszt arrangement of Beethoven's *Fifth symphony* for piano released in 1970 by CBS was more a curiosity than anything else. Arrangements, however, are common enough where a whole new instrumentation is involved (*ie* not merely a keyboard reduction) but, naturally enough, all the recorded sound will have originated from playing parts (used in the broad sense to include keyboard layouts) rather than from a score.

' The presentation of a record (as distinct from its individual contents) nevertheless has its own character, music is recorded for several reasons; the pieces may be offered basically:

i as a part of a composer's output (*ie* the *Mozart* operas, *Brahms'* songs, *Beethoven's* symphonies)

ii as a performance interpretation (*ie Klemperer's* Beethoven, *Callas'* Carmen, *Beecham's* Seraglio)

iii combined with other longer or shorter pieces to illustrate a performer's technical capacity (*ie* recitals by *Caruso, Kreisler, Rubinstein,* etc)

iv subordinated to the instrumental aspect (*ie* 'Virtuoso trumpet works ', ' Baroque recorder music ')

v as a subject, geographical, chronological or other pattern (*ie* ' The enjoyment of opera ', ' English music for strings ', ' Elizabethan part songs ')

vi as a reflection of the performer's (or performers') personality (*ie* all things ' pop ')

vii as part of the history of recording as such.'

LIBRARY CATALOGUING PRACTICE

Current discographical practice has been built up over a period of years by amateurs who are also highly expert in a limited field. This has largely been in the field of 78rpm discs, whose special problems have led to the development of specific techniques. In terms of institutional libraries the field of sound recordings is a relatively new one, and methods of cataloguing have been varied. A brief survey of the professional cataloguer's attempts to come to grips with the problem will provide a perspective for the consideration of the present state of the art.

Although one or two isolated examples of library use of commercially made sound recordings of classical music pre-date the outbreak of war in 1939, the main developments in this branch of librarianship have come about since 1945.

Originally there was a great temptation to catalogue a recording in the same way that one would a book, treating the label or wrapper as the title page, and transcribing it. Commonsense tended to prevail however. In 1939 the Music Library Association issued an *Interim report of the committee on the cataloguing and filing of phonograph records*[67] in which they said:

' Unlike books or music, records should be catalogued by the music they contain, without regard to their physical form.'

However, there was no cataloguing code for recordings until 1942 when the MLA published its Code.[68] This continued to emphasise the practical angle of approach as recommended by the MLA three years before:

' Unlike books or music, records should be catalogued by the music they contain, without regard to their physical form. Thus if there are two or more selections to one disc, each should be catalogued separately, since often there is little or no connection between them. . . .'

Since then four further publications have appeared, all of which give a different emphasis to the problem of dealing with recordings. These are:

Library of Congress. *Rules for descriptive cataloguing in the Library of Congress—phonorecords*. Preliminary Edition, 1952.

Music Library Association. *American Library Association code for cataloguing music and phonorecords*. 1958.

Library of Congress. *Rules for descriptive cataloguing in the Library of Congress—phonorecords*. Second Preliminary Edition, 1964.

American Library Association *and others. Anglo-American cataloguing rules: British text*. Library Association, 1967.

The Anglo American rules, while making many sensible and practical suggestions for such descriptive problems as imprint, collation, performers and edition recorded, falls down in the most important respect: the main entry. Going back on the pioneering wartime work of the MLA, and the precedent created by discographers all over the world, the code opted for the following for the main entry:

'A *Single works and excerpts*.

The entry for a work, or for excerpts from a work, recorded on a phonorecord or set of phonorecords is the same as the entry for the same material in its visual form. The applicable rules of entry for books and book-like materials (Chapter 1) and for music (230-232) are followed. In the case of popular music the indication of authorship on the phonodisc or other phonorecord may appear as follows : " Smith-Jones-Black " or " Words and music by Smith, Jones & Black "; in this event an arbitrary choice for main entry must be made, the final name listed being chosen as most probably that of the composer.

' B *Collections*.

1 With collective title. Two or more works by different persons issued under a collective title are entered under the title. If, however, a person or corporate body is prominently named as compiler on the label or other source from which the title is derived, entry is under the compiler.

2 Without collective title. Separate entries are made for each work when two or more works by different persons are issued together without a collective title. They are linked together by a " With " note in each case (see 252F11). Exception is made for works considered to be of slight importance, which may be named in an informal contents note (see 252F10).'

When dealing with a recording containing only one work this is fine, but when the record contains a collection of pieces, it will then tend to be entered under the catchy title given it by the manufacturer: ' Bravo! Sir Adrian '.

The problem is that of specific entry of everything in the recording. Some libraries will have circumvented this problem with unit entries or added entries or references, but it is a cumbersome and impractical method. However, it serves to highlight a major problem to the discographer—how to indicate couplings, and how far should these be repeated on each entry.

The above considerations are made even more difficult for collections of pop records, where access by title and artist is important. However, news comes of revisions to these rules in AACR67 as this study is completed, and clearly practical experience in the field will bring a new viewpoint.

DISCOGRAPHICAL PRECEDENT
From the beginning (in dealers' catalogues of records, early manufacturers' catalogues, and discographies) there were two factors of interest: the artist, and the work performed. From the viewpoint of the manufacturer the total disc was always of importance, although in the earliest recordings, of course, being single sided they rarely contained more than one item. Nevertheless even when records became double sided, customers were usually interested in one particular piece of music, the coupling being merely a bonus that one could not refuse. As far as discographies were concerned the objective was to catalogue what was available—the medium was not strictly relevant until one wanted to obtain the recording in question.

Numerical catalogues have been produced, but there is a limit to such undertakings, their principal interest being in seeing all the items issued on a particular label, their chronology and the existence of unissued items. Such considerations are really only of great value when dealing with 78s.

In an artist discography, particularly of an opera singer, the entry may be under the title of the opera, by aria, or by composer. In a compilation illustrating the career of the artist in question, the arrangement might also be in the order that the recordings were made. Occasional compilations have also been classified by record company, a procedure of particular value in the case of one company's product being of high technical quality, and another low.

In the case of J Dennis's discography of Tauber (*Record collector*, October 1969 p 182-183), where the basic arrangement is by company, an alphabetical title index was given as well as the following notes on discographical layout, which are of general interest and provide a convenient model for such things:

'A number has been assigned to each recording authenticated. This is followed by the matrix number and title, all on the same line; occasionally with a long title, translation or name of a partner this may run on to a second line.

'The line following the titling gives the issue numbers, where applicable single face numbers first, followed by double faced catalogue numbers, with precedence given to the country of first issue. Some recordings were issued in so many countries that these particulars may also take two lines. Microgroove re-issues are indicated in the last line, preceded by 33 or 45 as applicable.

'Couplings—with so many countries to contend with it would have taken too much space to indicate the coupling of every issue number, so this has not been included. Generally the coupling is adjacent or reasonably so and easily ascertained for any country of issue. Some widely separated ones are indicated in the text. The remaining contents of long play and extended play 45 re-issues are shown as discography numbers in the separate tabling at the end; the couplings for single 45s are not given.

'Layout—the recordings almost divided themselves into sections as Tauber made only 30cm acoustic discs, no 27cm titles have been traced. Then follow the 30cm German electrical recordings, the 25cm German electrics and the few Austrian and French discs of that size made in 1933-5. Finally the ten British 30cm sides followed by the 25cm. Within these limits all records are listed in matrix order, which is near chronological, though some take numbers indicate that the issued version was made at a later session than its immediate neighbours. An obvious case is the *On with the motley* from the film version of *I Pagliacci*, which with take 5 is dated as being five months later than Part I of the Prologue; but Part II, with four takes, is officially given as having been recorded at the first Pagliacci session. Where ascertained, recording dates have been inserted, regrettably few, but enough to give the collector a fair idea of when any recording was made.

'Accompaniment—as far as is known all opera and operetta titles are with orchestra. Songs actually checked show " w. piano ", or " orch ", etc. Catalogues and labels are not always correct with this information.

' Use of Umlaut—as capital letters A, O & U are not generally available here, where they should occur the alternative AE, OE & UE are used.

' Take numbers have proved quite a problem which is far from being solved. Many of the later RO and PO pressings appear with a take number one higher than the known original issue. In many such cases tested both have been shown to be from the same original recording and the author assumes that in such cases the take number was increased by one when the recording was " re-mastered " to add a run-in groove at the outer edge to make the pressings playable on auto-change mechanisms. In many cases though, two different takes have been issued. Distinguishing these is not easy as Tauber was able to sing remarkably similar versions of a song even at some years' interval, let alone at the same recording session. So to be certain the collector must possess not only both takes, but generally also twin turntables, one at least with variable speed and play the two together. Once accurately ganged together the result will either sound like one record, or with different takes like a duet; playing one disc immediately after the other is usually not conclusive. Tauber differed to the majority of prolific recording artists in that it was not until near the end of his career that he recorded on a royalty basis; previously he had always drawn cash for his recordings. One is therefore left wondering whether under these circumstances the management, like Edison, demanded more than one " perfect take ". Certainly with Tauber there are more cases of two takes being issued than with any other singer, proportionately to the fact that he recorded more than most, and at this stage one can only wonder why two or more perfectly good takes should have been made.

' The fact that no royalty payments were involved also explains why so many of Tauber's discs were re-issued under another number. If for instance recordings existed of songs used in a film, these were re-issued, together with new recordings of fresh material involved.

'It is remarkable that for a singer with such a vast output, only one serious unpublished title has been traced. Gaps in the matrix numbers suggest that many more titles were recorded.'

Where entry is made under aria or title of an opera, the composer's name (in the case of familiar music) is sometimes omitted in the cause of brevity. Not a practice to be condoned, although used in *Le grande voci*.

As far as composer discographies are concerned, the format will depend on the purpose for which the discography is being compiled. In WERM the compilers used two main methods of entry—alphabetical for short listings and a classified arrangement by genre for longer listings, with indexes as they were required. This is still a good basic philosophy.

Jerrold N Moore's *An Elgar discography* (BIRS, 1963) is chronological in arrangement, and this is of particular historical value in Part III 'Elgar's recording sessions'. However, the BIRS is tending to adopt a self-indexing alphabetical arrangement, and this has shown itself to be a functional and practical form of arrangement, but it does little except list the recordings and allow the reader to find them again. No new insights are gained.

A PRACTICAL DISCOGRAPHICAL ENTRY

In any catalogue of recordings the three important elements in each entry will be:

1 the work recorded;

2 the performer(s);

3 the manufacturer's issued number, and in the case of 78s, the matrix number.

Arrangement would therefore be by 1, sub-arranged by 2 (either in alphabetical or recording date order). The manufacturer should be abbreviated, and the size and speed of the disc given, and the matrix number as well as the issued number.

As far as 78s are concerned, where the recording was unique to a particular master, the repetition of any given performance under a new number may be immediately seen from the matrix number, and vice versa; the re-issue of a new performance (as happened with the Vaughan Williams's *Sixth symphony*, see page 41) under the same number may also be seen. Furthermore the matrix number can be fitted into a given point in time: the recording date. Therefore it is a far more reliable dating tool than an issue date, reviews or advertisements. Sample layouts illustrating these different approaches may be seen in illustrations VIII, IX, XI, XII, and XIII.

JOURNAL STYLE

It is wise in advance of completion of a given discography to consider how it is to be published: as a monograph, in a journal, or even (especially in the case of jazz discographies) as a privately published duplicated publication, reproduced from typescript. Indeed, with the ease and cheapness of short-run offset-litho printing, it is likely that more enthusiasts will use it as a medium of publication for their work. There are, in fact, a number of limited circulation journals produced in this way (see chapter XIV).

If the discography is to be offered to a journal for publication, the style of the proposed publisher should be borne in mind, or a draft submitted. There is nothing more annoying than to have the work accepted but have to re-type to someone else's specification at the last minute.

VII

TYPOGRAPHICAL STYLE AND ABBREVIATIONS

A glance at any published discography will immediately reveal the fact that a lot of information is most conveniently conveyed by typographic style, the use of symbols and of abbreviations.

TYPOGRAPHICAL STYLE

Definite styles have been established by the various publishers of discographies. Use of the full range of printing types (bold, italic, small capitals, and so forth) is really a necessity. However, in view of the range of type faces that is often called for, such printing can be expensive.

Typewritten compilations *can* be effective, but tend to be cumbersome. However, a lot depends on the ingenuity of the compiler and his typist. Claus Fabricius-Bjerre's *Carl Nielsen: a discography* (second edition, Copenhagen, Nationaldiskoteket, 1968) is a good model of what can be achieved. The main points to note about this particular publication are: firstly, the use of numbered entries; secondly, all entries are aligned to the left, subheadings and main headings being indicated by the use of broken and continuous underlinings respectively; finally, while the playing speed of any particular item is indicated (78, 45, 33) no indication is made as to the diameter of the recording, the compiler assuming that the user will be able to decide this information from the prefixes to the manufacturer's numbers. (See specimen page, illustration IV.)

The best models to be used in deciding upon a typographical style are *WERM, The Gramophone LP catalogue* and the various discographies published in *Recorded sound*. (See specimen pages, p 64-65.) However, it should be remembered that the specific typographic style peculiar to WERM is a copyright feature of that work.

COMPARISON OF STYLES

The compilers of *WERM* developed a layout that (in the main volume) did not have to take account of the difference between microgroove and coarse groove records, and did not try to indicate the diameter of

COMPOSER (Date of birth and death)
CLASSIFICATION where applicable.

GENRE or TITLE OF OPERA, etc.

Title of the individual item. Voice or instrumentation, date of composition, etc.

Name of Artist or Orch.—Conductor Main No.
(Number of sides or *coupling*)   (Subsidiary Nos.)

▲ Post-1936 minor recordings.

¶ Pre-1936 recordings, available in England in 1950.

§ Pre-1936 recordings, not available in England.
(except occasionally as imports)

H Recordings of historical interest.

SONGS are set out:

Title, Op. no. (Author of text)
(*Translation of title*, subtitles, etc.)

Singer & accompanist   Main No.
(*Coupling*)   (Subsidiary Nos.)

The ▲, ¶ & § sections are frequently subdivided according to language of performance, which, in the absence of special indication, is in the original language; and also in some cases, by accompaniment, etc. This also applies to operatic arias and vocal music in general.

Excerpts from a larger work (unless this is divided into numbered or other sections) are shown as follows:

...Adagio only

or as the case may be. An ARRANGEMENT of such an excerpt for some other instrument, etc. is introduced by a double dash, thus:

— — ARR. VLN. & PF. Wilhelmj

while a single dash

— ARR. ORGAN Best

refers to an arrangement of the whole work of which the title precedes.

NOTE—It can usually be assumed that the coupling given applies both to the main number and to subsidiary numbers, unless a different coupling is cited, or the notation d.c. indicates a different coupling. This does not apply where no coupling is given in the case of subsidiary entries, or to LP numbers. American album numbers are usually given as: "In set..."; but sometimes lack of space renders omission of "set" necessary.

In the coupling lines, the composers' names are always followed by a colon : to separate them from the titles, etc., while generally the name of an opera or other large work is followed by a dash — to separate it from the words of an aria or other similar excerpt.

Where no composer is named in the couplings, it can be taken for granted that the title on the reverse is by the same composer as the obverse ; except in the case of operas and similar works whose titles are well-known, where the composer's name would be redundant.

In the case of operatic lists, where neither composer nor opera is named on the reverse side, the title will be from the same opera as the obverse.

Generally, couplings are only given in shortened form, sufficient to guide the reader to fuller entries elsewhere.

the discs listed. Thus the only need for varying typography was to ensure clarity. Certain items concerning the dating of recordings listed were indicated by symbols and couplings were indicated in *italic*. Opposite is the ' diagram of setting out of the normal entry ' reproduced at the beginning of the main volume.

The first supplement to *WERM* saw the arrival of the first LP records and presented problems solved by more abbreviations:

In the Supplement the signs ▲ and § are no longer necessary; but we have saved space by the introduction of the following new signs:

♯ = Long-Playing records, 33⅓ r.p.m.

♭ = 45 r.p.m. discs or sets; as the set numbers, and frequently the disc numbers also, can be deduced from the 78 r.p.m. numbers, they are only listed in special cases.

♮ = Automatic couplings only (78 r.p.m. only).

☆ = Re-issue of a recording found in the main body of WERM. [1]

▽ = Entry omitted from WERM.

Numbers without the ♯ and ♭ signs are normal 78 r.p.m. discs, except for those prefixed PV. and FPV, which are 78 r.p.m. " Variable Micrograde " discs.

The sign ¶ appears rarely, and only to show that a British re-issue retains a pre-1936 number, instead of being re-numbered.

The use of ‡ has been extended to include the marking of re-used numbers by AmD. 20000 series). † refers to the *Anthologies* section of this Supplement.

DFr. re-issues on LP use the former 78 r.p.m. set numbers as the ♯ disc numbers, so we have not needed to re-list these.

Later, Clough and Cuming used a layout in their other published discographies that tended to break the recordings into two sequences —microgroove and 78rpm. For example in their discography of Vaughan Williams in *R Vaughan Williams, a comprehensive list . . .* (OUP 1961) they used the following:

† originally issued on 78 r.p.m.

§ 45 r.p.m.

‡ recorded at an actual performance.

* pre-electric recording.

In Part One all numbers not indicated as 45 r.p.m. (§) are 33⅓ r.p.m.

Records available in Great Britain at the time of going to press have their numbers printed in heavy type: **D.LXT 5143.**

Couplings are indicated by title, or name of composer, in italics: (*Benjamin*).

The word 'in' prefixed to a number denotes that the record contains short pieces, too numerous to list here.

Many of the records have been issued in countries other than those mentioned in the list of Abbreviations, but space does not permit the inclusion of the numbers allotted to such issues.

From the above it will be seen that even in the work of the same discographer the use of symbols and style need not be consistent. There is as yet no standard, and even if there were, technological change would soon render it out of date. In any work the symbols and style must be decided upon at the outset, and a list given at the beginning which must then be consistently followed.

Discographies of living composers that have been a feature of *Recorded sound* at the time of writing, for example that of Robert Simpson (July 1972, p 84) have adopted a format in which one alphabetical sequence is given. As the bulk of the material in such discographies has been located in the BIRS, the BBC Sound Archives or privately held, there has been no necessity for a complex typography, and the use of bold typeface in these compilations for the actual record numbers seems somewhat superfluous.

The record year 2 (by Edward Sackville-West and Desmond Shawe-Taylor, Collins, 1953) is probably the best example of the use of typographic style to designate the speed and diameter of the recordings in question. This was succinctly explained in the introduction to that volume (p 10):

' The lay-out follows, in general, that previously used; the main symbols are briefly listed on page 16. One important departure from previous practice has been forced on us by the ever-increasing number of record makes and prefixes. Since it is no longer reasonable to expect the reader to spot the make of a record by its letterprefix, we have begun each quotation with a maker's symbol, normally the initial letter of the company. An alphabetical list of these symbols is given on page 13.

' We have continued to use bold type for LP prefixes and numbers, ordinary roman type for SP (78); 45s are printed in italics. Letter prefixes in bold or roman CAPITALS show a 12-inch record; those in small letters a 10-inch. (All 45s are 7-inch.) The simple principle of using small or capital letters as a symbol of record size has encountered little opposition and much approval. When ordering records from a dealer, however, readers should remember to use the customary capital letters. They would also be well advised to add some brief indication of identity to the record number, since it is scarcely possible to keep a book of this sort quite free from numerical mistakes. We are still smarting under the reproach of the gentleman who last year ordered Schubert's C major quintet, only to receive an exotic mélange of assorted Braziliana by Villa-Lobos.

64

A M. Lympany & Nat. Sym.—Sargent (D.K 1467/70)
A. Schnabel & Chicago Sym.—Stock (Vic. 11-8416/9, set M 930)
W. Kempff & German Op. House—v. Kempen (Pol. 67674/8)

§ A. Schnabel & L.P.O.—Sargent (G.DB 1886/9; Vic. 7661/4, set M 156)
[7]W. Backhaus & R.A.H.O.—Ronald (G.DB 14.25/8)
[12]K. Szreter & Orch.—Weissmann (P.E 10533/6: P9059/62)

No. 5, E flat major, Op. 73 ("Emperor")
A. Schnabel & Philharmonia—Galliera G.DB 6692/6
(10ss)
C. Curzon & L.P.O.—Szell D.AX 282/6
(Swiss D.K 2281/5; Lon.T 5250/4, set LA 123; & LP: Lon.LLP 114; D. LXT 2506)
V. Schiøler & Danish Radio—Garaguly Tono.X 25098/102
(10ss) (Son.K 9534/8)
E. Fischer & Saxon State—Böhm G.DB 5511/5
(10ss)
W. Kempff & Berlin Phil.—Raabe D.CA 8248/52
(9ss—Bach: Wachet auf)[11] (Pol. 67082/6)

[13]B. Huberman & Vienna Phil.—Szell C.LX 509/13

(9ss—Bach: Unacc. Sonata No. 2, excpt)
[14]F. Kreisler & L.P.O.—Barbirolli G.DB 2927/32S

(11ss—Vic. 14163/8, set M 325)[15]
[14]G. Kulenkampff & Berlin Phil.—Schmidt-Isserstedt T.E 2016/21
(11ss—Mozart: Adagio, K 261) (U.F 22550/5; o.n. TE 496/501)

A.M. Strub & Saxon State—Böhm (G.DB 5516/21S)
[16]K. Freund & Berlin Phil.—Davisson (Pol. 15205/9)
[17]H. Merckel & Lamoureux—Bigot (G.W 1508/12)
[7,15]J. Szigeti & Sym. Orch.—Walter (C.LX 174/8; AmC. 680704D, set M 177; LOX 157/61)
L. Zimmermann & Amsterdam—Mengelberg (C.DHX 20/4)

§ J. Wolfsthal & Berlin Phil.—Gurlitt (Pol. 95243/7)
R. Queling & Berlin Sym.—Gurlitt (Od. O-6951/5)
F. Kreisler & Berlin St. Op.—Blech (G.DB 990/5; Vic. 8074/9, set M 13)

Egmont See Stage Works
Fidelio See Stage Works

Cadenza(s) by: [1] Clara Schumann [5] Kempff
[2] Pierné [6] Moscheles
[4] Saint-Saëns [8] Casadesus
[7] W. Backhaus [9] Anton Rubinstein
Other Notes: [8] At a radio broadcast on 29 Oct., 1944.
[10] Auto only.
[11] This coupling does not appear on recent pressings of Pol. 67082/65, according to the 1950 catalogue.
[12] In England, now Auto. only: DB 9011/5.

Cadenzas by: [14] Kreisler [16] Joachim
[15] Auer & Joachim [17] Leonard
Other Notes: [13] Re-issued Sept. 1946 with f.u. Scherzo from Qtt. No. 16.
[14] Re-issued Sept. 1946 with single-sided; re-issued Sept. 1946 with Kreisler:Tambourin Chinois on last side.
[15] Originally 14168 was single-sided.

I *Part of a page from* The world's encyclopedia of recorded music *showing the use of footnotes for detailed additional information. (By permission of F F Clough and G J Cuming, and Sidgwick & Jackson Ltd.)*

LP 775	Foote, Arthur 1853 - 1937	A night piece, for flute and string quartet. Julius Baker, flute; Sylvan Shulman, first violin; Bernard Robbins, 2nd violin; Harold Coletta, viola; Bernard Greenhouse, 'cello.
* LP 439		Suite in E major (1910). (F 18) see American music for string orchestra
LP 180	Foss, Lukas 1922 -	Behold! I build an house. Roger Wagner Chorale; Roger Wagner, conductor.
* LP 425		The jumping frog of Calaveras county, a comic opera based on the story by Mark Twain (1950). After Dinner Opera Company; Frederic Kurzweil, piano. (F 10)
* LP 405		A parable of death. Vera Zorina, narrator; Farrold Steven, tenor; Louisville Orchestra; Robert Whitney, conductor. (F 30)
LP 477		A parable of death (chamber version). Marvin Hayes, narrator; Richard Robinson, tenor; Pomona College Glee Clubs; Lukas Foss, conductor.
* LP 958		Piano concerto no. 2. Lukas Foss, piano; Los Angeles Festival Orchestra; Franz Waxman, conductor. (F 29)
* LP 180		Psalms. Roger Wagner Chorale; Roger Wagner, conductor. (F 40)
* LP 664		String quartet no. 1 (1947). The American Art Quartet. (F 32)
LP 1041	(Foster, Stephen)	A commemoration symphony. Mendelssohn choir; arranged and orchestrated by Robert Russell Bennett. see Bennett, R.R. (See also in Popular Catalog.)
LP 158	Franceschini, Gaetano	Trio sonata in B flat. see Instrumental music in Colonial America
LP 294	Gauldin, Robert	Pavane. Eastman-Rochester Symphony Orchestra; Howard Hanson, conductor.
LP 539	Gehot, Joseph	Quartetto in D major, op. 7, no. 6. see Instrumental music in Colonial America
* LP 605	Gershwin, George 1898 - 1937	American in Paris (1928). Morton Gould and his Orchestra. (G 1)
LP 56		American in Paris. Morton Gould and his Orchestra.
LP 474		American in Paris. see Levant plays Gershwin.

II *A page from the USIS catalogue* Recordings of music by Americans, *USIS August 1961.*

HISTORICAL

THE CREATORS OF GRAND OPERA. WORLD PREMIERES.
1877-1892 (MCK500). Massenet. **Le Roi de Lahore:** Promesse de mon avenir (**Jean Lassalle**, baritone Recorded 1902, Pathé Cylinder 2871). Sullivan. **The Martyr of Antioch:** Come, Margherita, come (**Edward Lloyd**, tenor. 1907, G&T 3-2855). Reyer. **Sigurd:** Sigurd, les Dieux dans leur clémence (**Rose Caron**, soprano. 1902, Zonophone 39027); Et toi, Freia (**Maurice Renaud**, baritone, 1902, Pathé 3386). Massenet. **Manon:** Oui dans la bois (**Georgette Bréjean-Silver**, soprano. 1906, Odéon 56210) Verdi. **Otello:** Esultate! (**Francesco Tamagno**, tenor. 1903, G&T 52673). Ora e per sempre addio (**Francesco Tamagno**, tenor. 1903, G&T 52675); Niun mi tema (**Francesco Tamagno**, tenor. 1903, G&T 052008); Era la notte (**Victor Maurel**, baritone. 1903, 1905, G&T 2-32814, Fonotipia 39042). Cellier. **Doris:** So fare thee well (**Ben Davies**, tenor. 1902, G&T 2-2781). Mascagni. **Cavalleria Rusticana:** Voi lo sapete, o mamma (**Gemma Bellincioni**, soprano. 1903, G&T 053018). **L'Amico Fritz:** Suzel, buon dì; Tutto tace (**Fernando de Lucia**, tenor; **Angela de Angelis**, soprano. 1917, Phonotype M2153); O amore, o bella luce (**Fernando de Lucia**, tenor. c1918, Phonotype M1703). Massenet. **Werther:** Pourquoi me reveiller (**Ernest van Dyck**, tenor. 1903, Pathé Cylinder 60604); Air des larmes (**Marie Delna**, contralto. 1907, Pathé 3512).

1892-1900 (MCK501). Leoncavallo. **I Pagliacci:** O Colombina, il tenero fido (**Francesco Daddi**, tenor. 1904, Columbia 10173). Bemberg. **Elaine:** L'amour est pur (**Nellie Melba**, soprano. 1906 IRCC 17). Puccini. **Manon Lescaut:** In quelle trine morbide (**Cesira Ferrani**, soprano. 1903, G&T

already for our Euclids ... Will it one day be possible to achieve it for our Davides, our Vellutis and our Fodors?". Well. Thomas Edison and his fellow-inventors did achieve it for us; and while the discs from the early years of this century could not in every case be called "an exact and lifelike record", anyone with the patience, and musicality, to learn how to listen to them can enjoy performances by great singers. from Patti onwards.

More: we live in a style-concious age. Think how much argument about appoggiaturas, about degrees and styles of decoration, would be resolved if Anna Strada and Gua lagni and Mozart's sisters-in-law had only made records for us! The early records are musicological documents of high importance. Here are the singers with whom Verdi, Massenet, Puccini worked. When I hear some young conductor today smash his way through *La traviata* with metronomic brutality, in the belief that by so doing he is "faithful to the score", I long to play him Violetta's first aria as sung by Gemma Bellincioni, whom Verdi

III *A review in* The Gramophone *in which the sources of an LP reissue of 78rpm records are closely documented. (By permission of* The Gramophone.)

SYMPHONIES

Symphony No.1, G minor, Op.7 (DF 16, 1891-92).

1. Danish Radio Symph.Orch., cond. Thomas Jensen. June 14-15, 1952.
33 m: Dec ACL 279. Dec LXT 2748. Lon LL 635. Phon LUPM 7004.

2. London Symph. Orch., cond. André Previn. Feb. 8-9, 1967.
33 m/s: Rca LM/LSC 2961. Rca RB/SB 6714.

3. Philadelphia Orch., cond. Eugene Ormandy. Feb.2, 1967.
33 m/s: Cbs BRG/SBRG 72606. Col ML 6404/MS 7004.

Symphony No.2, "De fire temperamenter" (The Four Temperaments), Op.16
(DF 29, 1901-02).

4. Danish Radio Symph.Orch., cond. Thomas Jensen. March 17, 1944.
78: Hmv DB 17-20, not issued.

5. Danish Radio Symph.Orch., cond. Thomas Jensen. Oct.3, 1947.
78: Hmv Z 7000-03.
33 m: Odeon KDO 2013. Odeon MOAK 30006 in the album CN 101.

6. Tivoli Concert Hall Orch., Copenhagen, cond. Carl Garaguly. Jan. 1960.
33 m/s: Fona LPK 510/SLPK 511. Fona PW/PWS 110. Tnbt TV 4049/34049 S.
Vox PL 12550/STPL 512550.

7. Chicago Symph.Orch., cond. Morton Gould. June 18, 1966.
33 m/s: Rca LM/LSC 2920. Rca RB/SB 6701.

Symphony No.3, "Sinfonia espansiva", Op.27 (DF 60, 1910-11).

8. Danish Radio Symph.Orch., cond. Erik Tuxen. Inger Lis Hassing, s.
Erik Sjøberg, bar. Oct.25, 26, and 30, 1946.
78: Dec AK 2161-65. Lon LA 126 (album). Phon HM 80005-09.
33 m: Dec LXT 2697. Lon LLP 100.

9. Danish Radio Symph.Orch., cond. John Frandsen. Ruth Guldbæk, s.
Erik Sjøberg, bar. March 3-5, 1955.
33 m: Epic LC 3225. Phil AR 00764. Phil NBR 6034. Phon LUPM 7005.

10. Royal Orch., Copenhagen, cond. Leonard Bernstein. Ruth Guldbæk, s.
Niels Møller, bar. May 16, 1965.
33 m/s: Cbs BRG/SBRG 72369. Col ML 6169/MS 6769.
Tape st: Col MQ 753.

11. "Bernstein prøver med Det kgl. Kapel" (B. rehearsing with The Royal Orch.).
Excerpts from 4th Movement.
Royal Orch., Copenhagen, cond. Leonard Bernstein.
45 st: Cbs 151265 a + b, non commercial.

Symphony No.4, "Det uudslukkelige" (The Inextinguishable), Op.29 (DF 76, 1915-16).

12. Danish Radio Symph.Orch., cond. Launy Grøndahl. Aug.17-19, 1951.
78: Hmv DB 20156-60.
45 m: Rca WHMV 1006 (album).
33 m: Hmv ALP 1010. Odeon MOAK 6 in the album CN 101. Rca LHMV 1006.

IV *Claus Fabricius-Bjerre's* Carl Nielsen, *2nd ed 1968. Note particularly the Nationaldiskoteket's clever use of electric typewriter, and the numbered entries.*

BREEN, J. Gavan (cont.)   A2237-A2239

   Clermont, Springsure,   1971   Bidjara   Biria
   Coomooboolaroo Station.   Wadjigu   Gongabula
   near Duaringa, Rockhampton,   Gangulu   Jandruwanda
   Stafford and Wacol
   (Brisbane), Qld.

   Clermont: Elicitation of Bidjara with Bob Martin
   and George Solomon. Springsure: Wadjigu with Mrs
   Amy Miller. A2238. Coomooboolaroo: Gangulu with
   Kruger White. Rockhampton: Biri with Reg. Dodd.
   Stafford: Gungabula (but possibly Bidjara) with Mrs
   Beatie Thompson. Wacol: Discussion of language
   names and territories with Benny Kerwin
   (Jandruwanta); elicitation of Jandruwanta. A2239.
   Jandruwanta cont. with story in language and English
   and two short songs by B. Kerwin.

CARROLL, Peter John   A2145-A2146

   Oenpelli, N.T.   1969-70   Gunwinggu   Erre

   Kunapipi song cycle, kudjika and djamalu sung by
   Gunwinggu performers (1970). A2146. Kunapipi cont.
   Erre language material by Magdalene Yarawaid (1969).

-----   A2147-A2149

   Oenpelli, N.T.   1970   Erre Urningangg
                                                    Amarag

   Erre language material cont. Uningangk language
   material by Elsie Gunbiriyag. A2148. Uningangk
   language material cont. Amurrag language material
   by Bendetta Guada. A2149. Amurrag language
   material cont.

DOUGLAS, Wilfrid   A2144

   Mullewa, Pindar Siding,   1968   Wadjari
   W.A.

   Mullewa: Watjari language material, vocabulary and
   songs, incl. men's and women's songs, some English
   conversation. Informants: Bessie Dingo, John
   Simpson, Ross Boddington, Queenie Dan and others.
   Pindar Siding: Watjari conversation, narratives
   and songs. Informants: Mr and Mrs Fred Simpson
   and Bill Hamlet.

V *Australian Institute of Aboriginal Studies* Catalogue of tape archive
   no 9, April 1972, showing entry under collector.

The Musical Underground:
A Comparison of Pirate Recordings (Continued)

STRAUSS: *Salome* (1905) ; libretto by Hedwig Lachmann after Oscar Wilde.
Ljuba Welitsch (s), Salome; Kerstin Thorborg (m-s), Herodias; Herta Glaz (m-s), Page; Frederick Jagel (t), Herod; Brian Sullivan (t), Narraboth; Herbert Janssen (b), Jokanaan; Deszo Ernster (bs), First Nazarene; Metropolitan Opera Orchestra, Fritz Reiner, cond. Recording of stage performance, March 12, 1949, Metropolitan Opera House.
EJS-158, 2 discs, mono, manual coupling. No libretto.
MRF-1, 2 discs, mono, manual coupling, in box. Side 4 contains a Welitsch interview and recital: Mozart: *Don Giovanni—Or sai chi l'onore; Sola, sola in bujo loco; Non mi dir* (c. Reiner, 1/6/51) ; Verdi: *Aida—Ritorna vincitor; O patria mia* (11/8/50). No libretto.

*

Ljuba Welitsch (s), Salome; Elisabeth Höngen (a), Herodias; Herta Glaz (m-s), Page; Set Svanholm (t), Herod; Brian Sullivan (t), Narraboth; Hans Hotter (b), Jokanaan; Alois Pernerstorfer (bs), First Nazarene; Metropolitan Opera Orchestra, Fritz Reiner, cond. Recording of a stage performance, January 19, 1952, Metropolitan Opera House.
SJS-701/2, 2 discs, mono, manual coupling, in box. No libretto.

*

(Incomplete recording): Gota Ljungberg (s), Salome; Dorothee Manski (a), Herodias; Doris Doe (a), Page; Max Lorenz (t), Herod; Hans Clemens (t), Narraboth; Friedrich Schorr (b), Jokanaan; Emanuel List (bs), First Nazarene; Metropolitan Opera Orchestra, Artur Bodanzky, cond. Recording of a stage performance, March 10, 1934, Metropolitan Opera House.
EJS-506, 1 disc, mono. No libretto.

*

(Fragments) Else Schulz (s), Salome; Mela Bugarinovic (m-s), Herodias; Joseph Witt (t), Herod; Paul Schoeffler & Hans Hotter (b), Jochanaan; Vienna Philharmonic Orchestra, Richard Strauss, cond. Composite recording of stage performances, February 15, 1942 and unidentified, Vienna State Opera.
EJS-463, 1 disc, mono. No libretto. Side 2 also contains fragments from Strauss: *Elektra* (Gertrud Kappel and unidentified singers, 1932) and Strauss: *Ständchen, Ich trage meine Minne, Morgen, Heimliche Aufforderung* (Julius Patzak, tenor; Vienna Philharmonic Orchestra, Richard Strauss, cond. Recording of concert performance, Vienna, September 15, 1944).

*

From the performance data, an intriguing batch of recordings—but in the listening vividly illustrative of the many problems endemic to "underground" discs that are not disclosed by the labels.

Consider first the most tantalizing: the fragments

(and they are no more than that—five-minute snippets taken apparently at random) that purport to be conducted by the composer. That the system from Vienna seems reasonably certain, for quite a large body of similar in-house material from the Staatsoper in the thirties and early forties is in circulation, bearing quite good credentials. But there has evidently been some hanky-panky here: in one excerpt, beginning near the end of the ensemble of the Jews (near No. 205 in the score), we hear the distinctive (and very distinguished) Jokanaan of Schoeffler, but further on, after an obvious and clumsy splice (following No. 220), he is transmuted into the equally distinctive Hans Hotter, whose name is not mentioned on the label. The only other well-known voice in this cast is Dermota's, and he is consistently recognizable as Narraboth—but clearly we have on this disc parts of two performances, which instills something less than perfect confidence in the label copy. For Vienna, sad to say, there is no equivalent of *Metropolitan Opera Annals,* or even of the less minutely detailed but generally useful histories of Covent Garden and La Scala—but by chance I have encountered a reliable listing of a Strauss-conducted *Salome* in Vienna on May 6 of the same year, with these same ladies, Joachim Sattler (Herod), and Hotter. Thus the EJS label's claims are not implausible, and perhaps a Viennese archivist, or the source of the original material, will come forward with further clarification.

Sorry about all that—but the purchaser who may be asked to fork over as much as ten dollars for this disc should be entitled to know whether he is getting what is "advertised," and should also be aware that ascertaining the true provenance of such recordings is by no means a

VI *Part of a review of ' pirate ' records from* The musical newsletter.
By permission of Patrick J. Smith. © *The Musical Newsletter Inc.*

6821-2 MERCHANT SEAMEN: Suite from Film. CONSTANT LAMBERT.   AOBR

BBC Symphony Orchestra, cond. by Constant Lambert.
(Boosey & Hawkes : Hire). 4 sides. 12′ 37″. 17.2.44. Recording prospectus M/DLO 50086

1. Fanfare (C) and Convoy in Fog   3. Safe Convoy (D)   ..   ..   3′ 42″
    (G flat)   ..   3′ 51″   4. Finale—March: Merchant Sea-
2. The Attack (E mi. ends E flat)   3′ 57″   men (D)   ..   ..   ..   2′ 47″

This music was written for the Ministry of Information film *Merchant Seamen.*

6823-4 OVERTURE: AGINCOURT (A). WALTER LEIGH.   AOBR

BBC Symphony Orchestra, cond. by Constant Lambert.
(O.U.P. Hire). 3 sides. 10′ 14″. 17.2.44.   Recording prospectus M/DLO 50086

1.   ..   3′ 33″   2.   ..   3′ 41″   3.   ..   3′ 6″

Walter Leigh was one of the composers commissioned by the BBC to write works commemorating the Silver Jubilee of Their Majesties King George V and Queen Mary in 1935. He composed this stirring overture, based mainly on the great song 'Agincourt', because it was his favourite of all English airs, and because it was about the King.

    Leigh was killed in action with the Eighth Army in North Africa in 1942.

See also note on the 'Agincourt Song' under 6892 (page 72).

6831 (a)   WHEN JOHNNIE COMES MARCHING HOME (C). Trad., arr.   AOBR
    Gordon Jacob.

BBC Variety Orchestra, cond. Charles Shadwell.
(MS). 1 side. 3′ 23″. 6.3.44.   Recording prospectus M/DLO 50740
A popular American marching song.

6831 (b)   O SUSANNA (G). STEPHEN FOSTER, arr.   Clive Richardson.   AOBR

BBC Variety Orchestra, cond. Charles Shadwell.
(MS). 1 side. 3′ 27″. 6.1.44.   Recording prospectus M/DLO 50740
One of Stephen Foster's popular songs.

6832 (a)   THE BAY OF BISCAY (B flat). Trad., arr. Gordon Jacob.   AOBR

BBC Variety Orchestra, cond. Charles Shadwell.
(MS). 1 side. 3′ 12″. 6.3.44.   Recording prospectus M/DLO 50740
A famous English sea song.

VII   *Part of a page from the BBC's Catalogue of special music recordings—
numerical catalogue with alphabetical index. BBC, 1945. Note detailed
layout with timings and sources given for the printed music.*

Session 23. 27 April 1926   Royal Albert Hall Orchestra   Queen's Hall, London

CR 332[1]△ [[1A]△]	'Cockaigne' Overture, part I (♯0-10)	D 1110
CR 333[1]△ [II]△	'Cockaigne' Overture, part II (♯10-20)	
CR 334[1]△ [[1A]△]	'Cockaigne' Overture, part II (♯10-20)	D 1110
CR 335[1]△ [[A]△]	'Cockaigne' Overture, part III (♯20-34)	D 1111
CR 336[1]△ [II]△ [[IIA]△]	'Cockaigne' Overture, part IV (♯34-end)	D 1111
	'Pomp and Circumstance' March No. 1	D 1102
CR 337[1]△ [[1A]△]	'Pomp and Circumstance' March No. 1	D 1102
CR 338[1]△	'Pomp and Circumstance' March No. 2	D 1236
	'Chanson de Nuit'	

VIII *Jerrold Northrup Moore's Elgar Discography, as originally published (BIRS, 1963) (above) and IX as revised (OUP 1974) (below).*

	MATRIX	SINGLE	DOUBLE
Pomp & Circumstance 4	AL8019f	2-0517	D 179[1]
Salut d'amour	AL8020f	2-0512	D 180[1]
	AL8021f	*destroyed ix.14[2]*	
Pomp & Circumstance 1	AL8022f	2-0511	D 179[1]
Bavarian Dance 2	AL8023f	2-0519	D 175[3]
Bavarian Dance 3	AL8024f	2-0530	D 176[3]

MOVING–PICTURE MUSIC

Seeger, Peter, May 3, 1919–
  [Rhapsody of steel. *Phonodisc*]
  Original sound-track music. [*Phonodisc*] Folkways Records FS 3851. [1961]

Tiomkin, Dimitri.
  [Rhapsody of steel. *Phonodisc*]
  Rhapsody of steel. [Pittsburgh] United States Steel [195–] matrix no. JB 502–503.

—EXCERPTS

Amram, David.
  [The young savages. Selections, *Phonodisc*]
  The young savages. Selections; an original sound track recording, a Contemporary Productions, inc. picture. Columbia CL 1672. [1961]

Amram, David.
  [The young savages. Selections, *Phonodisc*]
  The young savages; an original sound track recording, a Contemporary Productions inc. picture. Columbia CS 8472. [1961]

Arlen, Harold, 1905–
  [A star is born. Selections, *Phonodisc*]
  A star is born. Columbia CL 1101. [1958]

Arnold, Malcolm.
  [The bridge on the River Kwai. Selections, *Phonodisc*]
  The bridge on the River Kwai, from sound track of the Columbia Pictures production. Columbia CL 1100. [1958]

Arnold, Malcolm.
  [Homage to the Queen. Selections. *Phonodisc*]
  Homage to the Queen. RCA Victor LM 2037. [1957]

Arnold, Malcolm.
  [The key. Selections, *Phonodisc*]
  Music from the original soundtrack The key. Columbia CL 1185. [1958]

Bernstein, Leonard, 1918–
  [West Side story. Selections, *Phonodisc*]
  West Side story. Lyrics by Stephen Sondheim. Columbia OS 2070. [1961]

Black tights, an original soundtrack recording. [*Phonodisc*] RCA Victor International FSO 3. [1962]

Bliss, *Sir* Arthur, 1891–
  [Things to come. March]
  Things to come; march from the film music. London, Novello [1939]

Bliss, *Sir* Arthur, 1891–
  [Things to come. Suite] *Phonodisc*.
  Things to come; suite. Welcome to the Queen. RCA Victor LSC 2257. [1958]

Bliss, *Sir* Arthur, 1891–
  [Things to come. Suite, *Phonodisc*.
  Things to come; suite. Welcome to the Queen. RCA Victor LM 2257. [1959]

Blue Hawaii. [*Phonodisc*] RCA Victor LPM 2426. [1961]

Blue Hawaii. [*Phonodisc*] RCA Victor LSP 2426. [1961]

Boston tea party. [*Phonodisc*] RCA Victor LM 2213. [1958]

Boston tea party. [*Phonodisc*] RCA Victor LSC 2213. [1958]

De Paul, Gene, 1919–
  [Li'l Abner. Selections *Phonodisc*]
  Li'l Abner; the original soundtrack score. Paramount Pictures. Lyrics by Johnny Mercer. Columbia OL 5460. [1959]

De Paul, Gene, 1919–
  [Li'l Abner. Selections, *Phonodisc*]
  Li'l Abner; the original soundtrack score, Paramount Pictures. Lyrics by Johnny Mercer. Columbia OS 2021. [1959]

X *Part of a page from the Library of Congress: National union catalog 1958-1962, vol 52 Music & phonorecords. Part two: Subject index, Rowman and Littlefield Inc, NY, 1963.*

U-U: Unvergänglich-Unvergessen. A German Odeon series of historical re-issues, several devoted to Tauber. These are in 45 r.p.m. **e.p.** and 25 and 30cm. l.p. form, which is determinable from the number of titles they have (see separate index). In the body of the work the U-U "Folge" number is used, the records usually carry other numbers as well.

WRC: World Record Club, British E.M.I. 30cm. l.p. re-issue.
20000, 21000 and **29000** are German Odeon single 45 r.p.m. re-issues.
123000 are French 30cm. issues.
177000 are Argentinian 30cm. issues.
188000 are Italian or French 25cm. issues.
196000 are Argentinian 25cm. issues.
217000 are Polish 30cm. issues.
236000 are Polish 25cm. issues.

For Long Play and Extended Play re-issues see separate Appendix.
Reklame is a Dutch series, issued at a lower price, one side Tauber and the other Dajos Bela. The sides carry the original German issue numbers, irrespective of whether single or double face, those from the 0-8000 series being shown as A or B. The labels are in a variety of colours, the importers M. Stibbe & Co., Amsterdam.

THE RICHARD TAUBER RECORDS
German Odeon 30cm. acoustic, 1919-1926

1.xxB6439   Ständchen (Beines) rec. 26 June, 1919, w. piano.
Rxx 76754, 0-8031, AmO 5015.
2.xxB6440   Träume (Wagner) w. piano.
Jxx 81025, Rxx 76751, 0-8031.
3.xxB6441   Zueignung (R. Strauss) w. piano.
Jxx 81027, Rxx 76755, 0-8032.
4.xxB6442   Ruhe meine Seele (R. Strauss) w. piano.
Jxx 81028, Rxx 76756, 0-8032, AmO 5015.
5.xxB6443   MARTHA: Ach so fromm (Flotow) (M'appari-Air des larmes).
Lxx 80960, Jxx 81029, 0-9505, 0-8611.
33 Scala 827, Des.DLP 121, BI 1812.
6.xxB6444-1 & 2   DER EVANGELIMANN: Selig sind die Verfolgung leiden (Kienzl).
Jxx 81032, Rxx 80720, 0-8171, AmO 1007.
33 Scala 827, BI 1812.
7.xxB6445   I GIOIELLI DELLA MADONNA: Madonna unter Tränen (Wolf-Ferrari) (Der Schmuck der Madonna) (Madonna con sospiri).
Jxx 81031, Rxx 80723, 0-8026.
33 0-80959, TAP 313, U-U 156, HQM 1111.
8.xxB6446   PRODANA NEVESTA: Es muss gelingen — Hans Arie (Smetana) (Die Verkaufte Braut—The Bartered Bride).
Jxx 81030, Rxx 80748, 0-8027.
33 0-83391, Et. 466, 742, HQM 1111.
9.xxB6447   EUGEN ONEGIN: Was wird der nächste Tag (Tchaikowsky) Lenski's aria. No recit.
Rxx 80719, both this and No. 42 which see, were used on 80719 and 0-8171.

XI *The* Record collector's ' *Richard Tauber discography* ' (*by permission J Dennis*).

1928 *January–July*
HAYDN. Symphony no.
104 in D, 'London'
JBCO   H C1608–10/C7228–30*
                              V 35981–3
VERDI. Don Carlos – O don fatale;
Il Trovatore – Condotta ell'era,
Stride la vampa
Maartje Offers (contr), orch   H DB1158
                              H unissued
MOZART. Serenade no. 13 in G,
K525, 'Eine kleine
Nachtmusik'
JBCO   H C1655–6
                              V 9789–90
                              V 36283–4
PURCELL. The Married Beau –
Hornpipe
JBCO   H C1656
                              V 9790
                              V 36284
                    H m ALP2641(SLS796)
CASALS. Sardana
London School of
Cellos   Sp H AF207
                    H m ALP2641(SLS796)

May 8
BEETHOVEN. Fidelio –
Abscheulicher!... Komm
Hoffnung
Frida Leider (sop), orch   H D1497
                              V 7118
                    H m COLH132

XII *A page from Malcolm Walker's ' Barbirolli discography' (from*
Michael Kennedy's Barbirolli, *MacGibbon & Kee 1971, by*
permission of Malcolm Walker). Note chronological arrangement
of recording dates.

Bréjean-Silver (continued)

56072	Faust: Faites-lui mes aveux	Gounod
56073	Noces de Jeannette: Air du rossignol, 2nd part	Massé
560...	Belle au bois dormant: Reverie CR	Silver
56051	Romeo et Juliette: Madrigal (w. Affre)	Gounod

1906.

56205	Fra Diavolo: Voyez sur cette roche	Auber
56206	Bohème: On m'appelle Mimi	Puccini
56207	Manon: Je suis encore toute étourdie	Massenet
56208	Barbier de Séville: Air de Rosine, 1st part	Rossini
56209	Barbier de Séville: Air de Rosine, 2nd part	Rossini
56210	Manon: Fabliau	Massenet
56211	Noces de Figaro: Air du Chérubin	Mozart
56212	Mignon: Polonaise	Thomas
56213	Reine Topaze: Carnaval de Venise	Massé
56214	Rigoletto: Au temple où ma prière	Verdi
56215	Lakmé: Tu m'as donné le plus doux rêve	Delibes
56216	Lakmé: Les fleurs me paraissent	Delibes
86000	Barbier de Séville: Grand air	Rossini
86001	Faust: Laisse-moi contempler (w. Scaremberg)	Gounod

BREMER, Annie. (Soprano).

Black G. & T., Berlin, 1904.

43313	Alle Jahre wieder (7")	Xmas Song

BRESONNIER, Luisa. (Soprano).

Black G. & T., Milano, 1903.

53252	Bohème: Valzer di Musetta	Puccini
53257	Traviata: Ah fors'è lui	Verdi
53258	Traviata: Addio del passato	Verdi
53259	Rigoletto: Caro nome	Verdi

BRESSLER-GIANOLI, Clotilde. (Mezzo-Soprano).   (1872 Genève-1912 Genève)
(Debut: Genève 1891)

Brown Odeon, 1906.

36688	Carmen: Chanson Bohème (IRCC 5009)	Bizet
36708	Carmen: Air des cartes (IRCC 5009)	Bizet

BREUER, Hans. (Tenor).

Black G. & T., Bayreuth, 1904.

2-429...	Siegfried: Zwangvolle Plage (piano acc. by. Seidler-Winkler)	Wagner

81

XIII   *Bauer's* The new catalogue of historical records (*by permission of Sidgwick & Jackson Ltd*).

NAGACHEVSKY, N. I., Tenor—

B3994 {Chanson hindoue (Sadko—Rimsky-Korsakov) *Russian*
 N. S. Lukine (*Baritone*)
{Song of the Venetian guest. (Sadko—Rimsky-Korsakov) *Russian*

DB926 Naila Waltz (Delibes—Dohnányi) *Piano* Wilhelm Backhaus
C1969 Naila—Waltz (Delibes, arr. Doppler) Royal Opera Orch., Covent Garden
C2397 Naila—Waltz (Delibes, arr. Dohnányi) *Piano and Cinema Organ*

B3602 Naila—Waltz (Delibes, arr. De Groot) *Instrumental* Edith and Kevin Buckley
C2247 Naila—Waltz (Delibes) *Piano* De Groot Trio
C1263 Nancy's Fancy (Country Dance) (arr. Cecil Sharp) Mark Hambourg
D1277 Nanny (Lauder) (*Baritone*) Folk Dance Band
B3425 Napoli (Bellstedt) Cornet with Band Del Staigers with Goldman's Band Sir Harry Lauder
DA1054 Napulitanata (Nevin) In Neapolitan (*Tenor*) Tito Schipa
B4230 Narcissus (Nevin) *Cinema Organ* Sydney Gustard
B2819 Narcissus (Water Stenos—Nevin) New Light Symphony Orchestra
DA1101 Narrative, The (Film ; Rogue Song) (*Baritone*) Lawrence Tibbett

National Anthem—See God Save the King

NATIONAL BAND FESTIVAL, Crystal Palace (*cond. J. H. Iles*)
Massed Bands

BD285 {Grand March " Le Prophète " (Meyerbeer) (1935)
{Sing a Song (Iles) (1935)
BD286 {"Champion" March Medley, No. 3 (1935)
{Amen Chorus (Messiah—Händel) (1935)
B8028 {Chorale—" Belle Vue " (Iles) (1933)
{Glencastle—March (Hawley) (1933)
B8061 {"Champion" March Medley (Ord Hume) (1933)
{Lead, Kindly Light. " Sandon "} (1933)
B8229 {Excelsis—March (Fonfia) (1934)
{Jesu, lover (Aberystwyth) (1934)
B8230 {Champion March Medley No. 2 (1934)
{May-day Revels (cond. S. Cope) (1934)
B8245 {Tannhäuser—March (Wagner) (1934)
{William Tell—Overture (Rossini) (1934)
B8246 {Christians, awake! (1934)
{Lift up your heads (Messiah) (1934)
C2470 {Hallelujah Chorus (Messiah—Händel) (1932)
{Praise my soul (Goss); (b) Edwinstone (1932)

XIV *An example of wide setting in the 1936 HMV catalogue.*

Folklore (Fortsetzung)

Melodie der Völker (Italien)
30 cm, AR 70998 IU
Napoli (Melodie der Völker)
17 cm, AR 40212 CU

Neapolitanische Lieder
— Berühmte Tenöre singen neapolitanische Lieder
△ Caruso / Gigli / Martinelli / Peerce / di Stefano / Björling /
30 cm, RCA HR 211
Schipa / Valetti / Tagliavini / Lanza
25 cm, Elec. E 60720
Benjamino Gigli, Tenor
30 cm, RCA LM 2337-C
17 cm, RCA ERA 100

Mario Lanza, Tenor
Giuseppe di Stefano
(+ s. SaP Künstler: G. di Stefano: Neapolitanische Lieder)
— Funiculi-Funicula / O sole mio
Fritz Wunderlich
(+ s. SaP Künstler; F. Wunderlich)
— O grande sommo Dio / O sole mio / Ninna Nanna
— Benjamino Gigli, Tenor
17 cm, Elec. EP E 40076
— Santa Lucia
Fritz Wunderlich
(+ s. SaP Künstler: F. Wunderlich: Welterfolge großer Tenöre)
— Santa Lucia / Wiegenlied / Mutterlied
Benjamino Gigli, Tenor
17 cm, Elec. EP E 40075

Roma (Melodie der Völker)
17 cm, AR 40210 CU

Serenaden und Lieder
Mario del Monaco, Tenor
17 cm, Dec. VD 538
Sicilia (Melodie der Völker)
17 cm, AR 40214 CU

Sizilianische Volkslieder
Giuseppe di Stefano
17 cm, Dec. VD 1037
Venezia (Melodie der Völker)
17 cm, AR 40206 CU

Japan
siehe auch Allg. Folklore: Volkslieder der Welt
Song and sound the world around : Japan
17 cm, Phil. 427031 NE
UNESCO-Collection – A musical Anthology of the Orient
6—30 cm, BÄR. BM 30 L 2012/17

Jugoslawien
(siehe auch Balkan / Mazedonien)

Chormusik aus Jugoslawien
von Cossetto, Spoljar, Gotovac, Ferjancic
17 cm, Cam. CM 17007 EP
Chor „Joze Vlahovic", Zagreb / Emil Cossetto
Dalmatien-Slowenien (Melodie der Völker)
17 cm, AR 41184 CU

XV *The treatment of folk music in the Bielefelder Katalog.*

Symphony #0 in d

composed 1863-4 (lost), revised 1869
first pub. 1924 (ed. Wöss)
critical ed. (ed. Nowak) pub. 1^c68

(scherzo) Berlin SO--Fritz Zaun   (78: Victor 11726; C 2659; EH 844)

(Wöss) Concert Hall SO--Henk Spruit

Concert Hall CHS 1142 (rel. 5-52)   ARG 7-52 PHR
(E) Nixa CLP 1142 (rev. 6-53); (F) Classic 6225

(scherzo) Philharmonia Orch--Lovro von Matacic

Angel 3548 B♭ ½s. (rel. 9-56)

(orig. ms.) Amsterdam Concertgebouw Orch--Bernard Haitink (rec. 7-4/6-66)

Philips PHM 500131/PHS 900131 (rel. 3-67); n.n. 802724   ARG 5-67 JD
(E) AL/SAL 3602 (rev. 4-67); (G) 802724 LY

Symphony #1 in c

composed 1865-6 (Linz version)
recomposed 1890-1 (Vienna version)
Vienna version first pub. 1893 (ed. F. Schalk)
critical ed. of Linz version (ed. Haas) pub. 1939 (reissued by Nowak 1953)

XVI *Part of a page from J F Weber's discography of Bruckner (from the
     ' Discography series' no X).*

WOOD, Hugh (cont)

Comus: scenes from
*Jeannette Sinclair (s), Kenneth Bowen (t), BBC SO — Norman Del Mar

	BBC	TP	2 Aug 1965	21.05hr	886W

3 Piano Pieces (1963)
Susan McGaw — BBC TP 12 Sept 1965 17.10hr M521R

Quartet, Op 4 (strings)
Dartington SQ — BBC TP 5 Dec 1963 20.00hr M3W

4 Songs to love-poems by Christopher Logue
Maureen Lehane (c) & Dartington SQ — BBC TP 8 June 1966 15.30hr M855R2-5

Trio (fl, vla & pf)
Richard Adeney, Cecil Aronowitz & Philip Ledger — BBC TP 26 Oct 1965 20.43hr M59SW

Wand & Quadrant: (voice, cl, vln & vlo (Poems by Christopher Logue)
The Image of love grows; Bargain my love; In the beloved's face; Love do not believe
Maureen Lehane (c), Colin Bradbury, Paul Collins & Jennifer Ward Clarke
BBC TP 22 Aug 1964 19.10hr M93W

WOOD, Ralph Walter (b 1902)

Quartet No 2 (strings)
McGibbon SQ — B3C TP 14 Aug 1965 21.50hr 675R

XVII *Part of a page from the BIRS Music by British composers of the twentieth century. Note full details of the broadcast from which they were made is given.*

RHEINBERGER

—Zug der heiligen drei Könige
Chorus in German
Basilica Chorus—Pius Kalt
12"—PD-27107

[Sweelinck: Hodie Christus natus est]
Vision, from Op. 156 Organ
Paul Hebestreit (Paderborn Cathedral)
12"—PD-27128

[Meditationes—Tema variato]

RICHARD COEUR-DE-LION (1157-1199)

An English King who had ample time to write some energetic verses while imprisoned in France from 1193-1194. Richard the Lion-Hearted is unfortunately better known to the music appreciation student than to the amateur lover of music.

Ja nuns hons pris Song in French
Max Meili (t) & Fr. Seidersbeck (viol)
(in Vol. II) 12"—AS-18

[with examples of French Troubadours & German Minnesänger of the 12th & 13th Centuries]

RICHARDSON, Clive

London Fantasia Piano & Orchestra
Clive Richardson & Columbia Light
Symphony Orch.—Williams
12"—C-DX1204
Clive Richardson with Sidney Torch &
his Orch. 12"—P-E11451
Monia Liter with Mantovani & his
Orch. 12"—D-K1173

SPENSER, Edmund (1552-1599)
Epithalamion
Cpte. Read by Michael MacLiammoir
(6/69) TC1126
(Stanzas 1, 4, 5, 8, 10-13, 17, 19, 21-23)
Anth. Ian Holm (6/66) PLP1010
The Faerie Queen (excs.)
Read by Tony Church, Prunella Scales, Margaretta Scott, William Squire and Gary Watson
PLP1011
Book III, Cantos XI, and XII
Read by Michael MacLiammoir (6/69) TC1126
Hymne in Honour of Beautie
(lines 29-161)
Anth. Ian Holm (6/66) PLP1010
Sonnets from Amoretti
Most glorious Lord of Life
Of this World's Theatre
Anth. Ian Holm (6/66) PLP1010

STALLWORTHY, Jon (b. 1935)
Letter from Berlin, A (5/67) PLP1088
Anth. J. Stallworthy

STANLEY, Thomas (1625-1678)
Belle Confidente, La (3/65) PLP1015
Anth. John Stride
Chide, Chide (3/65) PLP1015
Anth. John Stride
Repulse, The (3/65) PLP1015
Anth. John Stride

STEPHENS, James (1882-1950)
Fifteen Acres, The (9/58) JUR-OOB1
Anth. Harry Hutchinson
Nora Griona
See: Misc. Ent. "The Barrow Poets" (8/63) PLP1072

STEVENS, Wallace (1879-1955)
Ploughing on Sunday
See: Misc. Ent. "The Barrow Poets" (8/63) PLP1072

STEVENSON, Robert Louis (1859-1894)
POEMS
Celestial Surgeon, The
Anth. David King (7/69) PLP1052
House Beautiful, The
Anth. David King (7/69) PLP1052

XVIII/XIX *Part of a column from The Gramophone Spoken word catalogue and the first (1936) edition of Darrell's Gramophone shop encyclopedia of recorded music. (By permission of The Gramophone and R D Darrell.)*

'Now that the same recording may be available in three different speeds, each differently coupled, the lay-out can reach an alarming complexity. We are sorry about this, but it is not our fault! We have tried to stick to certain rules of order, though we are aware that exceptions have crept in. As a general rule, long works are listed in the order: 33, 78, 45 (the last speed is of course seldom used for such works). Shorter pieces such as overtures or arias, which do not extend beyond two 78 (or 45) sides, are listed in the order: 78, 45, 33. 78 equivalents of new LP or 45 issues have been listed, even when the original recording is many years old.

'Fill-ups are shown, as before, in italics and square brackets beneath the record titles. When preceded by 33, 45 or 78, the fill-up applies to this speed only; otherwise, it applies to all speeds for which record numbers have been quoted. Often a work which has a fill-up at one speed will occupy the whole of a record (or set of records) at another speed. It has sometimes been necessary to vary the starring of the same fill-up in different speeds (thus: **78 and *45). These are cumbrous things to explain; but we hope that our practice will prove self-explanatory.'

The Schwann and Gramophone catalogues are probably the widest used record catalogues, and thereby have had a considerable influence on the layout of discographies. In the case of Schwann, there are few typographic indications of the nature of any particular recording. Bold is used for stereo, a dagger indicates 'other selections on record' which are unspecified. A diamond (♦) indicates a particular item is marked for deletion, while cartridges and cassettes are indicated by a triangle (▲) and a dot (●) respectively. The only respect in which Schwann is unique in such typographic usage is in the use of capital letters for major keys and lower case for minor keys.

The *Gramophone LP catalogue* makes similar provision. Apart from a dot (●) for a record marked for deletion and an asterisk (*) for a new listing, the following are in general use:

Index Letters	*Numbers*	*Example*	*Type of Record*
Roman Capitals	Roman	LPM18000	Mono LP
Bold Face Capitals	Bold	**ZRG5125**	Stereo LP
Reversed out	Bold	4	Tape cassette
		8	Tape cartridge

In particular the use of a capital R to indicate that a particular item represents a re-issue, should be noted.

There are no commonly accepted abbreviations for such terms as 'reissued', '78rpm', 'sides', 'coupled with', 'stereophonic', 'quadraphonic', etc. However, as can easily be seen, different discographers have solved such problems with a little typographic ingenuity, and their lead should be followed according to the needs of any particular compilation.

If a discography is not for publication in a journal or series with an established style, then great care should be given to the layout. Various specimen layouts should be experimented with, and before finally sending the manuscript to the printer, great care should be taken over the marking-up.

OTHER ABBREVIATIONS

Abbreviations for record companies often cause trouble, and the usage in the discographies we have described should be considered. There are particularly good lists of record labels and prefixes in both *WERM* and the *Gramophone LP catalogue*. The usage of 'Gramo' as an abbreviation for HMV (*ie* Gramophone Company) is not one that I personally condone although used by the British Institute of Recorded Sound.

As far as abbreviations for musical instruments are concerned, the British Standard on the presentation of bibliographical information in printed music[61] should be referred to.

Three problems are worth a final mention. Firstly, capitalisation of initial letters of abbreviations. I can see no need for it, but ensure consistency through any given compilation. Secondly, make sure the abbreviations for bass, bass-baritone and baritone are adequately differentiated, and finally the use of 'fag' (*ie* fagotto) as an abbreviation for 'bassoon' is widespread and may be preferred by some.

The only rules that can be made on this question are *be consistent* and *always give a guide to usage at the beginning of your work.*

66

VIII

ARRANGEMENT

We have seen there is a variety of ways in which the discographical compilation may be expressed on paper. The bald list is of limited use except as a finding tool: the way any discography is arranged should express the compiler's insight into the nature of the material.

Thus, for example, a discography of the Boston Symphony Orchestra could show the development of the orchestra under various conductors, and the influence of outstanding players. These factors and contemporary value-judgements could be used to assess the varying periods of the orchestra's existence, as reflected in a comparative hearing of the surviving record legacy, and the choice of repertoire and of soloist. Considerations of style at different periods could also be entertained. As in the case of Boston, a large number of unpublished archival discs survive, the best method of arrangement would be chronological with an accompanying commentary indicating the arrival and departure of personnel. It would need to be heavily annotated and archive recordings would have to be interfiled with commercial issues.

I hope that this brief hypothetical example has demonstrated the most important consideration as far as arrangement is concerned: *the task will almost always dictate the most acceptable arrangement,* and its effectiveness will depend upon the knowledge of the compiler. The following methods of arrangement are all possible:

1 Alphabetical, by author/composer, title or artist.
2 Classified.
3 Chronological.
4 Geographical/place of origin.
5 Manufacturer/company of origin.
6 Dictionary: an alphabetical listing in which artists, title, composers are filed in one sequence.

ALPHABETICAL
Alphabetical listings may be made for composer, title or performer orientated works. In considering an alphabetical arrangement two

points should be noted. Firstly, the spelling and usage of foreign names. Which titles will be expressed in English and which in the original language? In particular, how will words originating from non-roman alphabets be transliterated? Will, for example, Tchaikovsky, Tschaikowsky or Chaikovski be used? In such cases it is usually best to select a particular reference book and treat it as one's authority and follow its usage exclusively. My personal preference in this respect is for the *Everyman's dictionary of music* compiled by Eric Blom. The *Gramophone's* practical and sensible method is functional, if not correct to the last scholarly nicety.

Secondly, one should relate the length of the proposed work to the arrangement to be used. Alphabetical, while convenient, is clearly a very unimaginative arrangement for long and complex works, but ideal for short compilations that may be quickly scanned.

CLASSIFIED

A classified arrangement will often be the most suitable in the case of prolific composers who are heavily recorded. In the case of Beethoven, *WERM* uses the following scheme:

A Instrumental: 1 Piano; 2 Chamber Music; 3 Dances; 4 Orchestral

 B Stage Works
 C Vocal
 D Miscellaneous

In addition other sub-genres (Bagatelles, Serenades, Sonatas, Sonatas —Violin and Piano) are brought out as subheadings, thus making the arrangement much clearer visually.

It is interesting to compare this with the evolution of the arrangement used in the *Gramophone LP catalogue*. In the issue for June 1955, the following headings appeared under Beethoven:

Symphonies
Miscellaneous Orchestral
Concertos
Chamber
Quartets
Trios
Duos
Violin Sonatas
Cello works
Piano

Song Cycles
Lieder
Choral
Opera.

By March 1972, this had been clarified and reduced to a much more thought-out system (which incidentally had to deal with a greater sheer bulk of material):

I Orchestral
II Chamber
III Instrumental
IV Vocal and Choral
V Stage Works.

In this context 'Chamber' is used to mean music for two or more instruments. Other compilations have used the same term to mean music for three or more instruments, and adopted 'instrumental' not only for solo instrumental music but for solo instruments with piano accompaniment, and instrumental duos. The use of a general term 'stage works' is a sensible and practical procedure in the case of a composer such as Beethoven, where there are more than one sort of stage work, each category being somewhat small. In the case of a composer like Britten, for example, it might not work so well owing to the great bulk of opera, and a separate heading might have to be created for 'other stage works' which could include ballet, and incidental music. In the case of a living composer, of course, the problem arises as to where to list such things as incidental music to radio features and background music to films. I would consider the arguments in favour of some generic term to cover all such productions (for which 'other dramatic music' would suffice) overwhelming, unless of course, there is a vast bulk of any one other category to be listed, when a more specific term would be used.

Classifications of this sort are almost a necessity in such cases, and if the material to be organised does not suggest its own classification, then a model should be sought in a general discography, a major general reference tool, or a thematic catalogue of the composer concerned.

CHRONOLOGICAL
In compiling a chronological listing the primary task is to decide exactly what the chronology is. If of recordings, are matrix numbers to be used? Or are company records to be checked for dates of recording?

Will issue dates suffice? If the chronology is of the material recorded, what is the authority of the date order used?

GEOGRAPHICAL

Compilations of all material recorded in a particular country are most commonly seen as trade discographies. The Finns published a discography of all recordings issued in their country (Haapanen, Urpo : *Catalogue of Finnish records* 2 vols Finnish Institute of Recorded Sound, 1967, 1970) but such general retrospective lists serve little useful purpose. Of greater importance, particularly in the context of ethnic and folk material, is the list of material relating to one place. (See chapter XV.) Other groupings might be by country, for example, the discography in the second edition of Bacharach's *British music of our time* (Penguin Books, 1951 p 228-256) which is a list of all the music by British composers available on commercially made discs in 1951 in this country.

MANUFACTURER, COMPANY

The main impetus to compile comprehensive numerical lists, at least as far as 78s are concerned, is because studies of the numbering systems can reveal unissued material, while the history and development of the company concerned may also be traced. (See chapter II.) In some cases, the Vocalion label, for example, complete numerical lists still have to be compiled in an area which is largely undocumented. Much short-lived material of the greatest interest is scarcely known in such cases. Finally, of course, studies of the numbers used provide the means for dating recordings. There appears to be very little reason for compiling complete numerical listings of the major companies' LP output.

GENERAL ARRANGEMENT

All compilations should be preceded by a preface or introduction which explains the reason for, and aims of, the work in hand. The scope and sources used should be indicated. It is useful to know whether listings have been made from secondary sources, and where the actual recordings have been handled, or even heard. If a classified sequence is adopted, it should be described and a list of the abbreviations that have been used should be given. The discography should be dated, and this can most conveniently be done by signing the introduction or preface, thus: LEWIS FOREMAN, May 1973.

If material is listed from obscure or unusual sources, addresses and instructions for obtaining it are also valuable. Finally, if the work is really large, some form of contents list may be required, and an index, or indexes almost certainly so.

Acknowledgements to those who assist in the compilation are just good manners. They can appear at the beginning of a large work, but may be better at the end of a short one, where a typeface two or three point sizes below that used for the text is appropriate.

NUMBERING

The question of whether or not to number entries is a thorny one. They certainly make reference easy from other publications, but they can make for confusion if more than one edition of the discography appears and the numbering system is revised. If a classified layout is used then numbering may be best applied within each classified sequence.

INDEXING

Unless the discography is very short, is in alphabetical order, or is purely a finding list, an index or indexes are essential. Indeed, regardless of arrangement, time spent on any index will never be wasted; for the more ways a user can approach his information, the more quickly and expertly can he use the material. Certain subjects will demand short indexes to a particular area within a larger study. Thus alphabetical title indexes to Schubert and Wolf songs, Liszt piano music, *etc*, are almost essential. The indexes that are scattered throughout *WERM* are a case in point, and enormously enhance the value of that book as a general reference tool as well as a discography.

Otherwise indexes should give access by performer, in the case of composer listings, and sometimes by instrument. The latter is particularly true in the case of ethnomusicological work. In Dennis's long Tauber discography (*Record collector* October 1969), the introductory title index (p 171-182) is a necessity (see p 57-58) for quick access to the very complex listings.

All the varied methods of arrangement that have been discussed in this chapter, can best be applied by the common-sense question : *what is the reason for making this catalogue?* If there are not problems inherent in the nature of the material, then construct the arrangement around the major features and remember that alphabetical arrangements are to some degree self-indexing. Make the entries as full as possible and construct as many indexes as time, finance and necessity allows. If in doubt examine a few previous compilations in the field from the viewpoint of arrangement.

Jazz is a performing art, which had the good fortune to arise at exactly the same time as its means of preservation and dissemination appeared. So the two grew together, and recordings are an integral part of the cultural development of jazz. This was recognised from the first as Charles Delaunay attempted to show in his *Hot discography* (Paris, 1936). An arrangement which demonstrates the development of an art form and categorises its various styles is a positive contribution to the understanding of that art, and could be imitated with advantage in other fields. Delaunay's work is an object lesson to all discographers as to the potential value of their craft.

The discography of jazz is extensive and somewhat esoteric in that a good proportion of it is in journals that are not available through institutional libraries in the United Kingdom. In the United States, where jazz is more seriously regarded as part of their musical heritage, a number of major sources are available (see Langridge, Derek, *Your jazz collection*, Clive Bingley, 1970, p 45-47). As in most fields further work must derive from an intimate knowledge of the literature.

The arrangement of jazz is of special interest and has implications for pop music discographies and any other form where the music is likely to differ from performance to performance. The most important element will usually be the artists, and if either a chronological arrangement or an alphabetical one is used, there will have to be detailed indexing. A further problem arises from the extensive use of pseudonyms: a question that extends into the pop music field generally. Unless the same artist has recorded under more than one name, however, it is frequently a practicable procedure to use the widely used name and merely refer to the other in a note.

Of course, if the aim is to compile the discography of a particular artist, then an arrangement will be used that shows the material in the best light and will often reflect the biographical history of the artist concerned.

The use of composer-arrangements in jazz are unusual, but nevertheless may be called for, particularly when dealing with the more ' composed ' styles of the recent past.

POP-MUSIC AND MUSIC HALL

Like jazz all other popular musical styles reflect the *performer* approach. In the case of music hall, it is possible that an arrangement might be attempted based on a particular hall, sub-arranged chronologically or by artist, but the present writer has not seen such an arrangement.

Given the basic performer approach however, the treatment of each performer can vary. A chronological system has definite advantages in showing stylistic development. Arrangements by label, while they might have some point in the jazz field, are probably of little value elsewhere. It is a sad fact that an alphabetical arrangement by the titles of songs is probably the most favoured, making the compilation immediately useful as a finding list, and juxtaposing varying performances of the same piece by the same performers. However, Rust's discography of Bert Ambrose (*Recorded sound* January 1966, p 26-29; April/July 1966, p 79-87) is an invaluable example of how a chronological arrangement can demonstrate the development of an artist's career, and the importance of his associates.

ELECTRONIC MUSIC AND MUSIQUE CONCRETE

In April 1964 Hugh Davies could write: ' Music on tape has now been in existence for fifteen years. During that time more than 200 composers have composed more than 1,000 works using the medium of tape, ranging from complete operas to radio interval signals. Of these, more than 200 are background and incidental music for plays or films ' (*Recorded sound* April 1963 p 206). Since then there has been an explosive development in this field, but the only major discography is that which followed Mr Davies's remarks quoted above, followed by a supplement in the issue for April/July 1966. In this the basic arrangement is by recorded label, with a composer index. However, although in some contexts a simple composer arrangement could be identical in most respects to a composer-arranged discography of conventional music, there is the added complication of the studio (or corporate) authorship. Frequently a single disc will contain a large number of short pieces by a variety of authors, and in this respect an arrangement by label may have much to recommend it.

ETHNIC MATERIAL

Discography probably makes its most important contribution to scholarship in the field of ethnomusicology. ' Ethnomusicology could never have grown into an independent science if the gramophone had not been invented. Only then was it possible to record the musical expressions of foreign races and peoples objectively . . .' (Kunst, Jaap: *Ethnomusicology*. The Hague, Martinus Nijhoff, 1969, p 12.)

Clearly in this circumstance, in which most of the source material for a whole area of study is preserved and collected by the medium of the sound recording, the discographical treatment of the available material is very important. Bruno Nettl underlined this importance when he wrote:

'Along with bibliography the science of discography is increasing in importance to ethnomusicologists. The raw material of ethnomusicology is best preserved, after all, not in books but as recorded sound. Thus a knowledge of commercial recordings and the ability to locate non-processed field recordings in archives or private collections is an essential companion skill to bibliographic facility.' (*Theory & method in ethnomusicology*, Free Press, 1964, p. 54.)

In studying the discographical method most appropriate to such a specific field, an examination of the material is necessary. A number of arrangements are possible in general compilations, although other arrangements may be called for for specific purposes. The basic division that will cause differences of approach is between commercially issued recordings (which after all is the way in which most people will encounter such material) and privately recorded (that is archive) material. That the latter is the raw material of the science of ethnomusicology makes its arrangement of great importance.

Clearly the most important facet to be considered about such material for general purposes, is a geographical one. Users usually require a song or chant from a particular country or area or from a particular group or tribe in a particular area. The arrangement by which the Indiana University Archives of Folk and Primitive Music are classified demonstrates this point:

'... new indexing system. This indexing has a dual basis: 1—the comprehensive *Outline of world cultures* prepared for the Human Relations Area Files by George Murdock, and 2—an equally comprehensive index of the languages of the world which was developed in the Archives from *Les langues du monde* (1952 edition) by A Meillet and Marcel Cohen. Each collection is thus classified as follows:

1 Cultural area according to Murdock.

2 Language according to the Archives linguistic index.

The following is an example of these entries as they would be found on an index card:

324-325   F-95
Line Islands, Hendricks, 1950
OV6 – Line Islands, OCEANIA, American Polynesia
334 11 00 – Carolines, OCEANIA, Malayo-Polynesian, Polynesia.

This field collection, No F-95, is found on tape rolls 324-325. The collector's name is Hendricks, the collection date 1950. The cultural key is OV6, the linguistic key 034 11 000. In both the cultural area and the linguistic entries, the first entry, *ie* ' Line Islands ' or ' Carolines ', represents the lowest level of classification available in each system. The following name, in capital letters, represents the highest level in the classification system. Other levels in the system follow in descending order. The full system for public use consists of five card indexes:

1 Cultural area file according to classification system.

2 Language file.

3 Archives Tape Library in numerical order of rolls.

4 File of collectors, editors, transcribers, commercial recording companies, sponsoring institutions and expeditions. Alphabetically arranged within divisions.

5 General alphabetical index.'

(List, George: ' The Indiana University Archives of Folk and Primitive Music '. *Folklore and folk music archivist* Winter 1959, Spring 1960.)

This sort of scheme is widely used. For example the Phonogramm-Archiv in Berlin catalogues its recordings geographically with respect to cultures and tribes, in the same way. The recorded medium at Berlin, is identified by a colour code. Two additional files categorise the material by presentation (*eg* singer or instrument) and by genre (*eg* ' battle song ').

Clearly such considerations can be over-simplified. But an indication of the sort of questions to be taken into account when categorising such material may be seen from Donald Taylor's background notes and commentary on the music collections of the Anglo Colombian Recording Expedition 1960-61 (The music of some Indian tribes of Colombia, *Recorded sound* January-April 1968, p ii, later published separately) when he wrote:

' What to our ears may sound very simple may in fact be exceedingly complex; the subtle rhythmical changes of a drummer, the tonal variations of a singer, the whole quality and beauty of a music may be drastically over-simplified by ears unaccustomed to such sounds, like a westerner hearing for the first time the ethereal and barely perceptible tonal shades of Chinese ch'in music.

' The three records, consisting of six sides, are divided primarily into approximate environmental areas of music; two are mountain musics, two of lowland coastal riverine peoples, and the last two of Amazonian tropical forest dwellers. This last group represented by the Tukano living along the Piraparana has on one side individual or simple sound combinations of various sub-groups or tribes of this large linguistic group, and on the second side lengthy extracts of the more complex sounds during a Makuna-Tukano festival. One of the mountain areas, and one of the coastal riverine areas, notably the Sierra Nevada and the lower Rio San Juan are not strictly examples of tribal music, but include missionary, creole village, and negro music, and was arranged thus partly to show the process of musical change and to examine some of the implications of this. . . .

' The question remains: how do we come to understand the syntax of sound of a pre-literate culture, and how may this be done before its source disappears, before we no longer have in our midst the very means to an understanding. For the importance and significance of musical sound to these people is still very much a part of their daily lives. It may be as fundamental towards a closer understanding of a society as is its language, mythology, or religion.'

Clearly in such cases, the compilation of extensive indexes is the only answer, and perhaps the basic organisation becomes less important. Such indexes will often need to consider the following parameters:

1 Culture and area (broadly geographical)
2 Language
3 Collectors, editors, transcribers
4 Type (songs, instrumental music etc)
5 Instrument or medium.

It should be remembered that often classification by family or instrument (for example) is a good system. It might well be easier to trace the Colombian Kuizi sigi under ' flutes ' than its specific name.

Other more detailed analysis in specific cases may include such complex matters as arrangement by rhythmic patterns.

However, when dealing with commercially issued recordings, it is often more convenient to use the recording company as the point of entry. Wachsmann, in his 'An international catalogue of published records of folk music ' (BIRS *bulletin* Summer/Autumn 1960) filed under country, sub-arranging by record companies in alphabetical order. In his introductory notes Dr Wachsmann created a number of useful precedents:

' The material is divided into six sections. The first five are arranged geographically according to continent and the sixth contains anthologies of which the individual items are normally also entered in the appropriate geographical section. In the first five sections the countries within each continent are given in alphabetical order. We have followed *Whitaker's Almanack* (London) for 1958 (the year in which this supplement was begun) as regards their assignment to continent and their nomenclature.'

Alan P Merriam, in his *African music on LP* (North Western University Press, 1970) solved the problem by arranging by record label and listing in great detail. A large number of indexes then follow:

I Record companies and producing organizations
II Album titles
III Language of album or cover notes
IV Collectors, authors or album and cover notes, recorders, engineers, composers, photographers, editors, institutes, scientific missions, artists, producers
V Performing groups and artists
VI Song texts given in notes in part or in whole
VII Language of song texts: by individual bands
VIII Photographs
IX Places of recording
X Music type: by entire recordings
XI Song types: by individual bands
XII Origin of songs and instrumental pieces: by entire recordings
XIII Origin of songs and instrumental pieces: by individual bands
XIV Music instruments: by individual bands
XV Composition of singing groups
XVI Stylistic characteristics: by individual bands
XVII Tribal groupings: by individual bands
XVIII Song titles: by individual bands.

For the English discographer, Japanese music must present a typically difficult case, and its treatment in David Waterhouse's ' Hogaku preserved ' (*Recorded sound* January 1969, p 383-402), a select list of long-playing records issued by Japanese record companies of the national music of Japan, takes the functional way out and the records are again listed by company. In his introduction Waterhouse writes:

'The most immediate problem, however, is to know what is available, and even if one can obtain copies of the voluminous catalogues put out for commercial use by the Japanese record companies, the script is somewhat baffling to the uninitiated. In preparing the present list of serial numbers and romanised titles of records, I have therefore had in mind the needs of musicologists and archivists who have the ambition to collect Japanese recordings, but either do not have access to Japanese catalogues, or lack the means to read them. It is also hoped that specialists will find it useful as a check-list of desirable recordings. . . . It should be added that the readings of Japanese names, and even more the readings of titles of pieces of music, are extremely irregular, and I cannot claim to have been infallible or even consistent in this respect.'

The folk sections of the Schwann and Bielefelder catalogues might also be noted for an acceptable precedent as far as geographical arrangement is concerned.

SPEECH RECORDINGS

The three main categories of speech recordings tend to prescribe their own treatment. Firstly, 'art' works—poetry and the theatre. In this case the treatment is likely to be subject to the sort of considerations that are applied to music. Secondly, documentary works—interviews, reminiscences, news features. Lastly, recordings made as records of events in practical administrative circumstances—court transcripts, pilot/control and ship/harbour conversations, *etc.*

As far as literary recordings are concerned, the interest is normally going to be either in the author of the work recorded, or in the actor or voice heard. In their 'Dylan Thomas discography' (*Recorded sound* Summer 1961, p 80-95) Marie Slocombe and Patrick Saul made their main entries under the company concerned, interfiling archive recordings by the name of the archive. Thus we had:

Argo

BBC

British Council

Caedmon

Columbia

etc.

Within each heading the records were listed in numerical order. This basic numerical catalogue was then provided with four indexes:

1 Index of works, other than his own, recorded by Dylan Thomas as speaker or actor.

2 Index of works by Dylan Thomas on records.

3 Index of speakers who have taken part in recordings of works by Dylan Thomas.

4 Supplementary index of names of people and organisations concerned in recordings related to Dylan Thomas and his works.

Finally a small additional section lists records of translations and of musical settings of works by Dylan Thomas.

This detailed description of one short discography has been made because it exemplifies all the possible problem areas in such a work. By making the main listing by company or source the emphasis is put upon a catalogue to assist the user in obtaining access to the material, and provides a means for simply seeing what is on each disc. The emphasis has been put on the recording as an object, rather than placing the emphasis on the material recorded, in which case the medium becomes somewhat incidental, and although it has to be stated it is of peripheral interest when deciding on the arrangement. However, Slocombe and Saul have provided a wide range of indexes and in doing so emphasise the necessity for such means of access that the arrangement of the main body of the entries is unrelated to the material recorded.

When a more general compilation is required, then there are comparatively few models to use as aids. The arrangement in *The gramophone spoken word and miscellaneous catalogue* is obviously based on the experience of the classical music catalogue, adding to the main concept of author and artist others as they become necessary. Thus there are 11 sections:

Author index
Artist index
Anthologies index
Title index
Recordings in foreign languages
Recordings for children
Miscellaneous entertainment
Documentary
Instructional recordings
Sound effects
Demonstration and test records.

79

The major cause of trouble, and the source of much expenditure of time, is when dealing with commercially issued speech (particularly poetry) records in anthology format. The analogy is with collections of songs each by a different composer. Thus on one disc there may be anything from one to two dozen items, all requiring separate entries.

Solutions are either to list under the record label and number, with detailed indexes, or, particularly if the individual items are from named volumes of poetry, separate items of which appear in a variety of anthologies, to enter under the name of the collection (*eg* Larkin, *North light*), then list the contents, as one would the ' numbers ' in an opera (see p 48). Then all the references to that anthology could be simply listed below, and the entry would bear some relation to what the user might expect to find if he were looking for the same item in printed form.

DOCUMENTARY SOUND RECORDINGS

As far as recordings of *events* are concerned, the interest will inevitably be the subject matter of the recording or in the period of the material recorded. Thus the main filing order will usually be some alphabetical or dictionary system, but examples of chronologically arranged discographies such as Milo Ryan's *The phonoarchive at the University of Washington* (Seattle, University of Washington Press, 1963), in which a large collection of broadcasts presented by KIRO-CBS of second world war news material is preserved, usually allow an historical theme to be developed in the listings.

ADMINISTRATIVE RECORDS

In the field of court transcripts, air traffic control conversations and similar material, the ability to find a particular item quickly is usually of considerable importance. For a continuing collection, possibly with a limited practical lifespan, the best arrangement will almost certainly be by order of accession, closely indexed by likely finding terms. Practical procedures have been developed which have discographical implications in the legislative recording programme of the Tennessee Archives:

' The Archives established a simple system for filing the disks. Records for each house were numbered consecutively throughout the 75-day session. Numbers were affixed to each disk with plastic tape with the same number appearing on the filing envelope and on the index sheet. As a double precaution to insure permanent identification of the disk and to minimise the loss in case of its destruction, recording was done on one side only. Onto the other side the operator dictated a statement identifying the house, the number of the General Assembly, the disk number, and the date on which the recording was made. In this way loss of the filing envelope, index sheet, and even the plastic-taped number would not prevent accurate identification and the refiling of the disk in its proper place in the series. . . .

'But regardless of any shortcomings there may be in our present system, we feel that we have provided a new and valuable service to future generations of historians, political scientists, economists, and others who wish to study our legislative proceedings. No longer will these students have to guess what lay behind the bare bones of the legislative journals, nor will they have to search through contemporary newspapers for clues to the debates on the passage or rejection of a bill. In less than one and a half file drawers in the Tennessee Archives they can find the complete record of one session of the legislature, not as interpreted, digested, or reported, but as it actually happened and sounded.' (Alderson, William T: 'Legislative recording by the Tennessee Archives', *Bulletin of the BIRS* Autumn 1956 p 2-8.)

WILDLIFE RECORDINGS

One might well expect there to be some similarity in generally adopted arrangement between material of an ethnic origin and that of a zoo-logical origin. Interest is directed along similar paths—geographic location, song or ritual sounds, tribal or genetic groupings. However, the extant literature of bird and other zoological sound recordings reveals that a specific method of arrangement has developed that is totally unexpected, but widely used.

The actual size of such discographies tends to be small, and thus they are easily scanned. Arrangement tends to be by the collector of the recording, with an entry following which varies from very full, as in the following example from Boswall and North's 'A discography of bird sound from the Ethiopian zoogeographical region' (*Ibis* 109, 1967 p 521-533):

'NORTH, MYLES E. W. (1958). Voices of African Birds. One 12-inch, 33⅓ r.p.m. disc. Cornell University Press, Ithaca, New York State, U.S.A.

Includes 42 species, each preceded by a verbal introduction. The place and date of recordings is given on the cover. All names follow Mackworth-Praed & Grant (1952-55).

' Side 1 : Hammerkop Stork; Marabou Stork; Egyptian Goose; Tropical African Kite; Fish Eagle; Yellow-necked Spurfowl; South African Crowned Crane; Lichtenstein's Sandgrouse; Red-eyed Dove; Ring-necked Dove; Laughing Dove; Emerald-spotted Wood-dove; Green Pigeon; African Cuckoo; Red-chested Cuckoo; White-browed Coucal; White-bellied Go-away-bird; Silvery-cheeked Hornbill; Grey Hornbill; Red-billed Hornbill; Yellow-billed Hornbill; Ground Hornbill; Red-and-Yellow Barbet; Black-throated Honey-Guide; African Red-billed Buffalo-Weaver.'

' Side 2 : Spotted Morning Warbler; Nightingale; Robin-chat; Eastern Bearded Scrub-robin; Grey-capped Warbler; Croaking Cisticola Warbler; Moustached Warbler; Striped Swallow; Slate-coloured Boubou Shrike; Tropical Boubou Shrike; Black-headed Bush-Shrike; Black-headed Oriole; Pied Crow; Fan-tailed Raven; Superb Starling; Red-billed Buffalo-Weaver.'

Given the practice of making entries under the collector or author of associated printed material, broad classifications are of value, as in Boswall's 'A British discography of wildlife sound ' (*Recorded sound* April 1969, p 463-465), where an arrangement is adopted which gives four short sequences—Wild birds, Cage birds, Zoo animals, Insects.

However, the question of arranging references to such material so that they are accessible by zoogeographic regions, and also by species, must not be overlooked. Boswall's 'A world catalogue of gramophone records of bird voice ' (*Bio-acoustics bulletin* April/June 1961) originally appeared without any form of index, merely tables showing how many recordings had come from each zoogeographical region. Later, as a result of a critical review in the *Wilson library bulletin,* a geographic index appeared (*Bio-acoustics bulletin* January-March 1964). Other compilations have included a systematic species cross-index (*eg* Boswall and North *op cit*).

When dealing with such material, it is essential that a detailed introduction precedes the compilation, specifying the limitations of the listing, authorities followed in designation of areas and of species and also giving full sources of the material with addresses. The following is extracted from Boswall and North (*op cit*) and is a good example of what is to be expected:

' This paper is the third to be published of six projected papers each covering a zoogeographical region of the world. The aim is to bring together information about the availability of bird sound recordings, including those on published gramophone records, those in public sound libraries and those in private collections.

'The boundaries of the Ethiopian region follow Moreau (1964), who gives a map on p 280 and a description on p 251. In fact, however, all the discs in part 2 of this paper refer to the African mainland. Nothing has yet been published for the islands of the Ethiopian region. We see no object in defining the region in any more detail since, even in part 5 of this paper (the notes on unpublished recordings), the only references to any parts of the region away from the African mainland are to Ascension Island, the Seychelles, and Malagasy.'

' *The Discography*
The following list of 13 gramophone records (or sets of records) includes all discs published up to mid-1966 known to include the voice of at least one Ethiopian region species recorded either in the wild or in captivity.

' In presenting this paper we have been faced with certain difficulties over nomenclature. The " authors " use English names which we follow in the discography. Whereas those in standard use in East Africa are those of Mackworth-Praed & Grant (1952-55), however, the most widely-used names in South Africa are those of Roberts (1957). We have therefore used a system, described below, in which each English name in the discography can be related to the English and Latin name in the systematic cross-index of species.

' Since the works of Mackworth-Praed & Grant (1952-55) for East and Northeast Africa, and (1962) for the southern third of Africa, provide a complete list of all the species referred to in the discography, the species cross-index follows both their order and their nomenclature. In cases where the " author " of a disc uses a different English name from that given by Mackworth-Praed & Grant, we have added in brackets the serial number of that species in the species cross-index. The figures given after the species name in the cross-index refer to all discs in the discography on which the respective species are recorded.

' In some cases a mistake has been made by an " author " in the identification of a species. Here, the mistaken name has been placed in square brackets followed by an = sign and the name used by Mackworth-Praed & Grant.'

IX

SOURCES AND IDENTIFICATION

As we have seen, the main difference between the discographer and practitioners of other forms of bibliographic research, is that the information necessary to make an entry in any given compilation is frequently lacking from the actual sound-recording. It is not simply a question of transcription in a prescribed form, but of identification and then formalisation in an appropriate way. The situation is certainly better today than it has been in the past, because a lot of work has been done identifying doubtfully titled commercial recordings, and the catalogues and discographies in which these are listed have created examples and precedents that solve many difficult problems of identification. A vast range of discographical apparatus has appeared, and frequently it is possible merely to adopt someone else's identification. Thus *WERM,* the *Stereo record guide,* and the *Gramophone LP catalogue* are essential tools to any discographer. Sadly, most foreign commercial catalogues are not so punctilious, particularly about identifying the contents of recital records, and are often of little use for this purpose. A typical example is the blanket heading ' organ music ' under J S Bach to be found in Schwann, in which such collections are listed but not analysed.

Where an existing tool has provided indexes (*eg WERM*'s index of Scarlatti's sonatas in alphabetical order of keys) or identified cadenzas (*eg WERM*'s footnote to Beethoven piano concertos) they can be used as a first point of search. There are many areas here where such compilations, separately published, would be invaluable tools for the music librarian and discographer alike. The, as yet small, series published by the Music Library Association and by Information Coordinators of Detroit, are good starting points in their fields. A comprehensive index-discography of the cadenzas used in Mozart and Beethoven concertos would be an invaluable tool, and could be the basis of an integrated stylistic study, contrasting, for example, the approaches to the cadenza for Beethoven's *Fourth piano concerto* by York Bowen and Saint-Saëns.

Otherwise, individual composers apart for the moment, the major areas of difficulty resolve into: pre-classical music generally; Elizabethan music; The baroque period; and Russian songs. As far as 'old' music is concerned, a knowledge of certain basic sources is of great value. The most important are those cited in *The Gramophone LP catalogue*, whose abbreviations may be generally used as standard.

A number of these are easily and cheaply available and, for example, it is always useful to have a copy of *My Lady Nevell's book* and the *Fitzwilliam virginal book* to hand (both cheaply available from Dover Books), so widely are the contents arranged and disseminated in forms other than the original.

Secondly, access to other thematic catalogues and collected editions and denkmäler are necessary, and will involve the discographer either working in a large music library or attempting to build up his own collection in the area of his speciality. Clearly this is facilitated by knowing what is available, and Barry S Brook's *Thematic catalogues in music* (Hillsdale, NY, Pendragon Press, nd [1972]), and Anna Harriet Heyer's *Historical sets, collected editions and monuments of music: a guide to their contents* (Chicago, 2nd ed. 1969) are invaluable guides. Finally, the example of James Coover and Richard Colvig's *Medieval and renaissance music on long-playing records* (Detroit, Information Services Inc, 1964) is worthy of investigation.

It should be remembered, incidentally, that when an item has been reviewed in *The gramophone*, a fairly rigorous identification will be made. When dealing with United States issues, the index to reviews in *Notes* should help locate an authoritative review, although American reviewers in the record press tend to adopt a less scholarly approach. However, although only covering very few recordings the reviews of recordings in the *Musical quarterly* and other similar journals can be very thorough indeed.

The baroque period can cause considerable trouble owing to the fact that even the major composers are not always fully documented, and anyway new discoveries are being made. The fact that odd movements are frequently arranged as teaching pieces and concert encores, means that this is usually the principal cause of trouble. However, identifying such pieces as 'Gavotte'; 'Gigue'; or simply 'Adagio' is easier today than it once was, for the reasons of precedent stated above.

As far as Russian songs are concerned, the problem is one that affects all works in languages that use non-Roman alphabets. However, in the case of Russian, the long established use of French in the nineteenth century, and in addition the wide dissemination of publications of German publishing houses means that there are often an embarrassing range of possible titles for any given piece. The British Standard on transliteration cannot be said to have provided a viable solution, because it introduces transliterations which while grammatically and phonetically accurate are at great variance with current usage, and worst of all affect alphabetisation in a dramatic way. There are of course two sides to the problem. Firstly, that of working out what a given English or French title really means, and secondly of actually transliterating a Russian label. For the latter there is no solution but attendance at a transliteration-for-cataloguing course.

X

DESCRIPTION OF SELECT DISCOGRAPHIES

In essaying a brief description of a variety of discographies in this chapter, the aim has been to show the methods and achievements in three specific areas:

1 The general critical record guide.

2 The regularly-published current discography used as a guide to availability by trade and collectors alike.

3 Guides to the discographies of specific performers on a general basis.

GENERAL CRITICAL RECORD GUIDES

In 1951 Edward Sackville-West and Desmond Shawe-Taylor set the pattern with their *The record guide* (Collins, 1951) for a whole series of publications that have appeared since in the UK and elsewhere. *The record guide* attempted a broad guide to the ' serious ' music available at the very end of the 78 era. The arrangement is by composer. A brief but stimulating note about each composer is followed by listing under the following headings:

1 ORCHESTRAL MUSIC
   Symphonies and Symphonic Poems
   Concertos
   Concert Overtures
   Miscellaneous
2 CHAMBER MUSIC (in decreasing number of players taking part: *eg* from Octet to Violin Sonata)
3 SOLO INSTRUMENTAL MUSIC
4 OPERAS
5 ORATORIOS, CANTATAS, CHURCH MUSIC
6 SONGS

Brief descriptions and interpretations of individual works are given and comments are made when there are competing versions of the same work, sometimes even referring back to deleted and unlisted versions. Outside the main alphabetical sequence there are also:

Addenda (August-December 1950); LP Records; Suggestions for a beginner; Alphabetical list of performers. The latter is particularly valuable.

The guide was selective at the time of issue, and a starring system to indicate recommended recordings is used. However, as a retrospective tool it is valuable. Valuable too for a number of introductory paragraphs that can be very useful, notably:

1 'Society' issues [a comprehensive listing] (p 20-22).

2 List of record prefixes and a brief note on lettering systems.

3 Miscellaneous special issues [references to records issued by Schott, Paxton, Neglected Masterpieces Recording Co., Collectors Corner].

The 1951 volume was supplemented by two volumes of *The record year* (Collins, 1952 and 1953). The original volume was then revised and published again by Collins in 1955, with a supplement in 1956. All are valuable for their commentary, but the original volume is especially valuable for its contents in addition to the critical listings.

After *The record guide* a number of short selective guides to music on record appeared of which Martyn Goff's three volumes (*A short guide to long play* (Museum Press, 1957); *A further guide to long play* (Museum Press, 1958), and *LP collecting* (Spearman, 1960)) are most readable if elementary, and very dated by now. At the time of publication Robert Simpson and Oliver Prenn's *Guide to modern music on records* (Blond, 1958) was a very good idea, being a survey of the contemporary music of each country with reference to what was (or often what *ought* to be) recorded. At the time it was valuable and all the essays are still most readable, and informative documents as an indication of the state of musical knowledge at that time, at least as far as twentieth century music is concerned.

However, the next concerted attempt to publish a comprehensive guide to the available serious music on record with indications of ' best version ' and so forth, came with *Music on records: a critical guide*. Written by Peter Gammond with Burnett James this readable survey in which the considerations of the works in question and the merits of varying versions of the same work are discussed at considerable length, was originally published by Hutchinson in four volumes (1962 and 1963) and later issued in paper covers by Arrow Books (1963 and 1964) in five volumes. The basic arrangement is by form, separate volumes being devoted to Orchestral music, Chamber music, and Opera & vocal music.

At the time of writing the two most important surveys of this type are the *Stereo record guide,* originally started when stereo records were a novelty rather than the norm, but now expanded into a comprehensive self-renewing body of comparative criticism on the available recordings in the UK, and rather similarly, the *Penguin guide to bargain records.*

The stereo record guide by Edward Greenfield, Robert Layton, Ivan March, Denis Stevens; edited by Ivan March. Blackpool, The Longplaying Record Library Ltd.

Vol I (1960) p 1-316
Vol II (1961) p 317-660. The text cross-refers back to vol I.
Vol III (1963) p 661-1102
Vol IV (1966) p 1103-1558. (Includes mono numbers for the first time)
Vol V (1968) p 1-321. A-Mc
Vol VI (1968) p 661-1026. Me-Z
Vol VII (1972) p 1027-1330. A-Ma
Vol VIII (1972) p 1331-1611. Me-Z

Originally conceived as a series to which additions could be made, but later as the volume of deleted stereo records grew, the series was revised. The result is a cross indexed series in which records may be reviewed more than once. The introduction to Vol VI stated : ' Volumes V and VI offer a current reassessment including records which were originally reviewed in Volumes I and III. Page numbers are included to refer readers back, where appropriate, to Volumes II and IV which remain a necessary part of the overall survey.' A useful feature is the inclusion of Mood music, Light music and Music for dancing, at the back of the first four volumes. This series has managed to maintain continuity longer than any other comparable attempt. For this, at the very least, it is notable and of value.

Penguin guide to bargain records by Edward Greenfield, Ivan March and Denis Stevens. Penguin Books.
Originating as *A guide to the bargain classics* (Long Playing Record Library, 1962-1965 3 issues) this guide is arranged on a similar basis to *The stereo record guide.* Since 1965 it has appeared as a Penguin in paper covers. Three issues have appeared 1966-1973, and between them the three paperback issues review all the ' bargain ' priced records to be issued in the UK over the previous ten years.

The discography of currently available records that is published at regular monthly or quarterly intervals is of importance to the trader, the record collector and the librarian alike. Of the various discographies of this nature that are published throughout the world, the three most important are those published in the UK—*The Gramophone LP catalogue;* in the United States—the *Schwann record & tape guide;* and the West German catalogue, the *Bielefelder Katalog.* The discographer who requires comprehensive listings of records by artists and composers over long periods will find it necessary to build up sets of these tools. It is not always necessary to obtain every issue, but certainly they should be taken at regular intervals, say six or twelve months. It is then possible by searching the set to pick up the majority of recordings in any given field of interest, at least as far as the regular commercially available companies are concerned.

The Gramophone long playing classical record catalogue. The Gramophone, 1953-. A quarterly catalogue continuously cumulating and published mid-March, June, September and December.

Title has now changed to: *Gramophone classical record catalogue.* The two major sequences are the composer index, the most scholarly listing in any published gramophone catalogue intended for day to day commercial use, and an artist index. A list of subscription sets and special issues is of value, as is the introductory list of record prefixes and addresses of companies. In connection with one of the four attempts that have been made to computerise the catalogue, the March 1966 issue was designated 'master edition' and issues appearing for the next two years only covered new material issued during this time. A final cumulation did not appear until December 1968. Apart from the classical catalogue The Gramophone also issues:

Popular record catalogue 1955- (later published in two parts: Artist section; Title section).

Spoken word and miscellaneous catalogue 1964-

Recommended recordings, a selective listing of items that have had good reviews in *The Gramophone* 1966-

Note should particularly be taken of the fact that the *Classical LP catalogue* acts as an index to the appearance of reviews in *The Gramophone* magazine, something that no other catalogue does.

The compilation of the *Gramophone LP catalogue* is undertaken as a hobby by its editor, Stanley Day. It is interesting to compare this procedure with the compilation of the Schwann catalogue—the one formalised with a permanent staff, the other a one man job, part-time. Its compilation is, in the main, based on records received for review by *The Gramophone*. This, in itself, provides a fairly comprehensive listing, but it is supplemented by information received from manufacturer's information and from personal contact.

First the compiler receives the 'record sheets'—the typed review headings from The Gramophone office—about two months ahead. Occasionally the information proves to be not completely accurate owing to an issue being delayed and so a record gets listed when it has not in fact been issued. Such listing of unissued material is a point for the discographer to be wary of. Equally, very occasionally some material that was commercially available was never listed even though issued and reviewed elsewhere, a typical example being the Herald recording of the Harty *Piano concerto* (HSL 106). However, it should be noted that the popular catalogue is not nearly so successful in achieving near comprehensive coverage. Strict numerical lists are kept to enable a check to be kept on the entry of all new issues. With the large companies this is done from their own lists. However, in the case of material that is reviewed briefly in the 'Nights at the round table' feature, the items are not listed, and resource has to be made to the annual index to the magazine in order to trace them. The cataloguing procedure grew from its own precedent. 'It's just common sense,' said Mr Day.

The problem of the division between popular and classical means that one is never sure whether certain 'middle of the road' items are listed appropriately. When the catalogue was broken into two parts there was left a group of records that were 'light' music. Liaison continued between both catalogues, and the entries rated by deciding the market that the record was aimed at. Some miscellaneous concerts of popular music are indexed in the artist section of the *Classical catalogue,* but not in the main list. All such listings are artist orientated, as they are usually artist-market orientated. The problem continues to exist that the catalogue is growing too large, and in spite of reductions in type size and adoption of triple columns, it is beginning to border on the uneconomic. Morgan[47] has indicated that if this happened there may be some possibilities of its function being taken over by the BNB in conjunction with the BIRS as a sort of current national discography (which it is in fact).

The major entries are divided into five classes which are chosen on the basis of the personal preference of the compiler. There are five now, but there used to be many more (see page 68-69). The present format is simpler to use and to compile than the previous more complex and cumbersome one. Errors are picked up by correspondents and users of the catalogue. Spelling by and large uses British/American usage rather than French, particularly in Russian names (eg U not OU). Inconsistencies in the use of foreign names means that there is what Mr Day calls 'practical inconsistencies'—the sensible approach is always adopted. There have been a number of changes in typography—always getting smaller, and in 1973 a lighter typeface was adopted.

Schwann record catalogue, Boston, Massachusetts, Schwann, 1949-. Title later changed to *Schwann long playing record catalogue* and now *Schwann record and tape guide*. Published monthly. Very first issue which was reproduced from typescript has recently been issued in facsimile.

The main listing is 'serious' music by composer. At the back, listings are given by album titles for collections, music shows, current popular and jazz. A good list of US record labels, numbers and prices is given. New listings each month are in a separate section.

Schwann also publishes other catalogues at irregular intervals:

Supplementary catalogue [listing of imports and other records not listed in the monthly catalogue].

Artist issue [currently available repertoire by performers].

However, the supplementary catalogue has now been expanded to contain all mono records as well as the more obscure material, and it appears regularly at six-monthly intervals. The monthly catalogue is now colloquially known as 'Schwann—1' and the semi-annual supplement as 'Schwann—2', and these designations appear on the covers.

Bielefeld, 1960-. Published twice a year.

Originally published as *Der grosse Schallplaten Katalog* (Das Langspielplatten-Verzeichnis für den Fachhandel) Hamburg, 1953-1959. This catalogue was familiarly known as 'Die Langspielplatte'. It then became the *Bielefelder Katalog*.

The catalogue is published in one composer sequence, with useful appendices of title indexes to operas and musical shows (in German, of course—itself a useful tool), a list of collections and of folk music arranged by country. Practice is generally nearer to the Schwann practice of not bothering fully to itemise all collections rather than *The gramophone* one of conscientiously listing very fully.

GUIDES TO THE DISCOGRAPHY OF SPECIFIC PERFORMERS
In this section it is proposed to treat the general guides that have appeared dealing with singers, rather than other specific items on certain composers. In this respect it is proposed to deal briefly with three such guides here: firstly Bauer's *Historical records,* secondly Kutsch and Riemens' *A concise biographical dictionary of singers,* and lastly Celletti's *Le grandi voci.* As the latter has assumed such an important place in this field it will be dealt with first, and the other two referred back to it.

Celletti, Rodolfo *ed : Le grandi voci : dizionario critico-biografico dei cantanti con discografia operistica.* . . . Rome, Istituto per la Collaborazione Culturale, 1964. 1044 cols.
A dictionary of singers with extensive discographies appended. Illustrated by 48 pages of plates. The main text is set in double columns. After a main alphabetical sequence, two further sequences are given, arranged in alphabetical order of opera titles, covering complete recordings and selections. ' Pirate ' recordings and LP transfers of 78s are included.
The philosophy behind this publication may be seen from the following brief extract translated from the preface:
' The importance of the record now as a document, whether it be the vocal or interpretative value of the most famous lyric artists—or of the stylistic evolution, even involution—as one can see in the field of opera from the end of the nineteenth century up to today, has in fact prompted the idea of publishing a dictionary limited only to singers who have made records of operas.'
The most important factor to remember about this publication is that while its discographies are not exhaustive, they are fairly comprehensive, and include all manner of ' pirate ' discs and unusual LP reissues. There is also a large catalogue of complete operas on records arranged by opera. The major drawback from the viewpoint of the English user is that it is exclusively in Italian, and is very expensive (£15.00 at the time of writing).

Kutsch, J and Riemens, L: *A concise biographical dictionary of singers*. Philadelphia, Chilton Book Co., 1969. (A translation of *Unvergängliche Stimmen: kleines Sängerlexikon*. Revised edition, Berne and Munich, Francke Verlag, 1966).

While not really a discography, but a biographical dictionary of singers, similar in style to Celletti, it is of great value to those dealing with vocal recordings. Brief accounts of the lives and careers of the artists are followed by very abbreviated discographies or guides to sources or recordings, the sole qualification for listing being the fact that the artist recorded. In the original there are 950 entries giving dates, present activity and a note as to the scope and quality of the singer's voice and the record companies for which the singer recorded. The 1966 German edition contains more entries than the 1962 and in the translation it is expanded again. Also the discographical information which was previously very brief has been expanded in the translation. The value of this volume is the large number of minor names that are included. However, the discographical information is no more than a guide and it is no substitute for another source if such a source exists for the singer required.

Bauer, Roberto: *The new catalogue of historical records* 1898/ 1908/9. Sidgwick and Jackson, 1947, 1970.

Originally published in 1937 under the title *Historical records*, this is retained on the later edition as cover title. The second edition appeared in 1947 and was reprinted by photo-litho in 1970.

' In this second edition of *Historical records* will be found record-listings of all internationally famous opera and concert singers known to have made lateral cut discs during the years, roughly from 1898 to 1908/9, as well as record-listings of other important vocalists whose reputations never travelled, for one reason or another, beyond the confines of their own countries.

' Collectors who compare this edition with the original catalogue of 1937 will note that a few names have been dropped and many others have been added. . . . Record-listings of certain vocalists whose reputation rested solely upon their recordings and not upon public appearances have been either eliminated entirely or reduced in length.'

Thus Bauer indicates the limitations of his catalogue, in his foreword. As a guide to both singers and record labels it is an invaluable compilation, but now very much out of date, even for the period it covers. Of particular interest is the use of a key lettered a to k to indicate when a particular artist recorded for a certain company at a given period. The importance of any given performance is at least partly indicated by the use of the symbol CR to indicate that the singer in question created this part in the world premiere of the opera. The layout may be seen from illus. XIII, but note should be taken of the division of the entries by label, and the style of the abbreviated entries. At the back of the book there is a very brief listing of instrumentalists.

XI

ADP AND BIBLIOGRAPHIC CONTROL

A subject such as discography and the cataloguing of recordings, in which a relatively large number of separate entries are required owing to the rate of change of the material available, but in which each entry can be comparatively simple and short, was an obvious candidate for the application of some form of mechanised handling of the information. There are two sides to this question. Firstly, the compilation by ADP means of commercially published current catalogues of records available. Secondly, the compilation of composer and performer orientated discographies, which could be a byproduct of such techniques, although not an integral part of such an operation. This would come about either from a national computerised discography or from the cataloguing by ADP methods of a major institution such as the BIRS.

COMMERCIALLY PUBLISHED DISCOGRAPHIES

On the face of it, it would seem that the commercially published finding list, such as The Gramophone catalogues, would be early in the field of experimenting with ADP for the easy and cheap production of their catalogues. While a simple and limited listing, such as *Pop singles* (Christopher Foss Catalogues, 34a Paddington St, London w1) has been successfully compiled and printed using punched cards, it is only after several attempts that *The Gramophone LP catalogue* has been successfully mechanised, with magnetic tape as its file medium.

The Gramophone catalogues, particularly those of ' classical ' music and speech recordings, are the most comprehensive consistently produced and they thus have two important implications for any future development. Firstly, if such catalogues were to become uneconomic, the trade would suffer a serious setback, although it might well be in the interests of the major companies, and to the detriment of the smaller firms. Secondly, the precedent of these listings, which perform the function of a national current discography, has considerable implications for any other listing that might follow covering similar ground. At least in the field of commercially issued recordings the items listed are identified by numbers, although an attempt is now being made to produce unique international numbers for records.

The Schwann catalogue has been converted so that ' the printing will be handled by electronic data processing and phototypesetting equipment. The conversion began with the Fall 1971 supplementary catalog which was prepared with the use of a Digital Computer PDP-10, a Fototronic CRT, and an ECRM Optical scanner.'[49] Schwann —1 has been prepared this way since the late summer of 1972.

THE BRITISH INSTITUTE OF RECORDED SOUND

The stock of the BIRS is large. Some 200,000 discs, 1,500 cylinders and 5,000 hours of tape are held, and are being added to all the time. However, there is no catalogue in the accepted sense. Catalogue information for the discs held is transcribed from the labels and written in manuscript on paper slips. ' There is a plan to convert the slips, at present filed in chronological order—one for each recorded item, and probably amounting to about 300,000 the detail on which is extensive—into machine-readable form using an adaptation of the MARC system developed by the British National Bibliography whose council has come to an agreement with the BIRS for the necessary pilot study; it is expected that this will make possible the publication of cumulative discographies based on the Institute's holdings '.[47]

Clearly the sort of format that is adopted by the BIRS can have considerable implications for a future national discography, if that ever proves feasible. The major difference being, at least as far as the lay user is concerned, between a page looking somewhat like *WERM* or *The Gramophone LP catalogue,* and one more reminiscent of the Library of Congress catalogue cards.

However, the advantage of having a large file of material that could be easily analysed would be considerable. In particular, it would enable the compilers of discographies relating to specific artists, to be sure of picking up the more obscure recordings of their subjects, particularly where the artist was not playing a major role, but as member of a chamber group, or leader of a section of an orchestra.

LIBRARY CATALOGUING MECHANISATION

The gradual development of computerised cataloguing methods for the bookstocks in libraries has provided a basis of experience for extending it into the audio-visual field. The problems have largely been ones of standardisation of the methods of making the entry, the cataloguing code to be used, in short, cataloguing problems rather than computer problems as such.

Collections of sound recordings have until now been the cinderellas of the library world. They have in the main only been established and kept going by enthusiasts, in the face of acute shortage of resources, and as a result anything approaching full bibliographic control has been lacking in most cases. ' There appear to be relatively few major collections in the United States which have complete control over their holdings. The hope offered by centralized cataloguing and cooperative projects in computerized systems is somewhat dimmed by the problems of establishing a format to serve the many needs of users of recorded sound.

' Some of these problems may be traced in the discussions of the draft of the MARC II format for sound recordings as reported in the pages of the Music Library Association's *Music cataloguing bulletin* ' (May, June, September, November and December 1971). 'Walter Gerboth believes that the highest priority should be placed on those parts of the system which permit retrieval by subject content. He also believes that parts of the draft format ' overstepped the bounds of cataloging and entered the field of discography '.' (*Ibid*, June 1971). ' If the MARC II format follows current Library of Congress cataloging practice it will incorporate many features of the Anglo-American cataloging rules which are clearly unacceptable to many discographers and many music librarians. James Coover was disturbed to learn that manipulative programs will not be available to MARC II users, and said ' we face the prospect that, in writing our own programs for our own special uses, we will end up with a proliferation of incompatible programs, mired in the kind of mess in which the sciences now find themselves '.' (*Ibid*, p 3). ' Coover suggested that basic programs developed by Barry Brook in conjunction with Rilm offer ' our only real hope '.' (Gordon Stevenson).[49]

The major advantage that one requires from a mechanised system is an ability to handle a mass of information in greater detail than would be feasible in a manual system. Occasionally this is found in organisations using manual methods, but this is rare in the field of sound recordings. Although their catalogues have not been published, two institutions which have produced unusually high quality local controls should be mentioned. James Coover wrote of the card catalogue of the 5,000-disc collection of the Music Department of Vassar College: 'The quality of that cataloging is exceptional. For almost every recording, cataloging was done by actual audition with score in hand, and the call number of that score was put customarily on the record catalogue card. In the case of works whose scores were difficult to locate, for those appearing in *Denkmäler* or in appendices to literary studies, for example, even the precise page number was added to the call number on the record card. In many instances, variants among several performances of the same work, and their corresponding scores, were noted.' (*Notes*, March 1969, p 437-446). Another catalogue, said to be of unusually high quality, is the catalogue of the Historical Sound Recording Program of Yale University, which includes matrix numbers, analytics, and other material not provided for in the typical 'library style' cataloguing.[49]

Initially the most important advances as far as the application of ADP techniques to cataloguing records are concerned will probably come about as a result of co-operative acquisition and cataloguing schemes. In this respect the Birmingham Libraries Co-operative Mechanisation Project is an excellent model, owing to the fact that attention is being given to music and sound recordings as well as to books. (*See* S W Massil: 'Music in an automated cataloging system using MARC', *Brio*, Spring 1973, p 1-4.)

A BRITISH NATIONAL DISCOGRAPHY BY ADP METHODS
There is clearly a need for a national discography. While *The Gramophone* listings of recordings of 'serious' music are very full in coverage, listings of other material is very haphazard. Probably pop-music is the worst single medium served by bibliographic services. There are a number of historical reasons for this, all to do with the snobbery that has given the major discographical tools their coverage. This is very strange when the origins of discography and its techniques owe a very large amount of work to collectors in the field of jazz. Symptomatic of this attitude is, of course, the fact that the BIRS covers pop music so thinly, and even then mainly with foreign material. A national discography would cover all material equally and so would provide an important record for the cultural historians of the future.

Probably the most important single question to be answered in considering such a compilation is the source of the information upon which the compilation is to be based. In an area where there is no deposit law, there are clearly very considerable problems. Of course, assuming that such a project could be successfully launched, and it seems likely that it could, who would buy it? While *The Gramophone* and other commercial catalogues successfully continue, this would appear to be the major area requiring market research, although outside the scope of the present author.

The whole question of non-book materials and the success of the *British national film catalogue* which has been produced by computer from March 1972, has led to the necessity for the establishment of some central agency dealing with media matters. 'At present, in the United Kingdom, non-book catalogue provision is inadequate both for the education service and for wider spheres in:

a comprehensiveness of coverage;
b sophistication and standardisation of catalogue detail;
c frequency of publication and speed of up-dating.

Recent developments in computer techniques offer a way forward towards improvement of this situation. It is the need to create this computerised bibliographic facility which underlines the concern of the National Council for Educational Technology (NCET) in this area. In the creation of the proposed system NCET is working very closely with the British National Bibliography (BNB) which already produces its catalogues via computer methods. This co-operation will continue when BNB becomes part of the British Library.

' The system will involve the effective co-operation of several existing catalogue-producing organisations and a central co-ordinating unit will be a necessity. We are actively discussing the form and structure of this central agency—tentatively designated British Media Record (BMR)—and examining the financial implications of the computerised system.... Initially, outputs from the data base will correspond to the current pattern of catalogues, but, subsequently, new catalogues could be prepared from the machine-held data to meet previously unfulfilled information needs (*eg* select subject listings, bibliographies, on-demand listings for individuals etc).' (A B Phillips, ' The British media record ', *International Cataloguing*, April/June 1973, p 6.)

The fact of a MARC format suitable for application to all forms of audio-visual media, means that sound recordings may well be able to join the general bandwagon of the current vogue for media materials, particularly in teaching, and thus achieve a properly established national bibliographic control formerly denied to the whole field. Alternatively, the computerisation of the entries involved with the *British catalogue of music*, may look forward to some form of joint listing. Either way the eventual outcome looks to be promising, although unlikely to be achieved in the short term. But the subject is under discussion which is the main thing.

XII

DEALERS IN OUT OF PRINT AND UNUSUAL MATERIAL

The second hand record trade is almost as well developed as that for books with the exception of the auction. There is a relatively small number of dealers and once the initial contacts have been made it is surprising what second hand material can be found. As well as 78s and out of print LPs there is now, and to an increasing extent, records of a non-commercial character that turn up in all sorts of lists.

The following brief directory of the more specialist and enterprising dealers will often bring to light even the more obscure 'wants'. To any discographer the mailing lists of such firms are almost vital to enable him to be fully aware of what material is, or has been, available.

UK DEALERS
78s only

Collector's corner
63 Monmouth Street
London WC2
> 78s are no longer the major trade of this dealer. Nevertheless a good source for unusual items, lists infrequent but well produced.

James H Crawley
246 Church Street
Edmonton
London N19
> Very wide stock advertised through duplicated journal called *Vocal art*. Also lacquer copies of very old discs.

Disco Epsom Ltd
45 Burgh Heath Road
Epsom
Surrey
> Some general lists, also lists devoted to specific artists.

Sir John Hall Antique Records
Carradale
29 Embercourt Road
Thames Ditton
Surrey
  Lists in periodical *Antique records*. Wide stock with many rarities.

Gramophone Exchange
80-82 Wardour Street
London w1
  Varied stock, no lists.

J Jarrett
10 Fernhill Road
Olton
Solihull
Warwicks
  Lists in his periodical *Record advertiser,* mainly vocal and very
  cheaply priced.

The Old Record
1a May Road
Twickenham
Middlesex
  Recently established shop : some lists.

The Record Collector's Shop
17 St Nicholas Street
Ipswich
Suffolk
  Proprietor of *The Record collector* magazine.
  Good vocal lists and books on record collecting and singing.

The 78 Record Exchange
9 Lower Hillgate
Stockport
Cheshire
  Good lists covering classical, vocal and instrumental, brass bands
  and popular.

Robert White
46 Millheuchbrae
Larkhall
Lanarkshire
Scotland
Very reasonably priced stock from vocal lists seen.

Winston,
32 The Upland
Ruislip
Middlesex
Good lists at moderate prices, including a few instrumentalists.

LPs from rare and unusual sources, including imports

Anglo-Russian Music
16 Manette Street
London W1
Imported ' Melodiya ' LPs from Russia. Lists issued.

Collets Folk Shop
70 New Oxford Street
London W1
Good coverage of jazz, folk and some ethnic material.

Discivio,
9 Shepherd Street
London W1

Dobells Folk and Jazz Record Shops
75 & 77 Charing Cross Road
London WC1
Jazz records including imports.

Gramophone Exchange (as above)
Wide selection of unusual LPs, especially imports. No lists.

Harlequin Record Shop
201 Oxford Street
London W1
Wide selection of mainly pop records including many unusual issues.

London Music Shop
218 Great Portland Street
London W1
   Stock includes imports, particularly East European. No lists.

Record Hunter Ltd
27-29 York Road
Waterloo
London SE1

Michael G Thomas
54 Lymington Road
London NW6
   Proprietor of *Rare recorded edition*. Good source for all out of the
   way issues.

Woodbridge Record Shop
4a Cumberland Street
Woodbridge
Suffolk
   Very good lists of imports and unusual LPs, particularly of LP
   reissues of 78s.

OVERSEAS DEALERS
USA

Barclay-Crocker
Room 8574
11 Broadway
New York 10004
   Pre-recorded reel to reel tapes; catalogues issued.

Darton Records
160 W 56 St
New York 10019

The DomArt Collection
126 Fifth Street
Providence
Rhode Island 02906
   Operatic 78s and LPs; lists issued.

Four Continents Book Corpn
156 Fifth Avenue
New York 10010
    Particularly good for Russian records.

Mr Tape
PO Box 138
Murray Hill Station
New York 10016.

The Record Lair
119 Lodi Street
Lodi
Wisconsin 53555.

Theo's Records
PO Box 4994
Panorama City
California 91412
    Soundtracks, personalities and jazz.

OTHER COUNTRIES

Bongiovanni
Via Rizzoli
28E-40125
Bologna
Italy
    Rare and unusual records; catalogues issued.

Discor
Treinta y Tres 957
Buenos Aires
Argentina
    Rare 78s; catalogues issued.

Vieux Phono
6 rue Vintimille
Paris 9⁰

XIII

SELECT LIST OF UNUSUAL AND SPECIALITY RECORD LABELS

Although the short history of the long playing record has seen a vast expansion of the recorded repertoire, the efforts of the major companies have been supplemented during the last ten years or so by the activities of a growing number of small organisations. In particular these are concerned with the following fields:

1 Reissues of 78s and cylinders, often including material that has not passed out of copyright and therefore must be considered 'pirated'. A vast range of very early recordings have been dubbed, often in competitive versions which allow the recording quality to be compared in the reissues.

2 'Pirated' material, usually from ex-broadcast tapes or acetates. The material is of the utmost historic importance, although the firms issuing it are often very difficult to find, owing to the fact that they are in breach of copyright and performing rights regulations.

3 Legally made recordings, usually by small organisations often in support of a particular artist or composer, or featuring amateur or semi-amateur forces.

The criteria for compiling the following is that they are not generally listed in the commercially published record catalogues, and are therefore very difficult to trace. There is no guarantee of their continued availability.

AD PORTEM Germany Orchestral works by Abel.

AMERICAN LISZT SOCIETY Radford College Radford Virginia.

ARIES Los Angeles Ex-broadcast stereo orchestral recordings, including Havergal Brian's *Gothic symphony*.

ASCO Reissue label, same organisation as TAP.

ARNOLD BAX SOCIETY 26 Rutland Court Queens Drive London W3. One mono LP to date of Bax's chamber music.

BARBIROLLI SOCIETY 8 Tunnel Road Retford Notts. One speech record of Barbirolli issued to date.

SIR THOMAS BEECHAM SOCIETY 664 South Irena Avenue Redondo Beech California 90277. Recordings of ex-broadcast Beecham performances.

BELCANTODISCS—Bel Canto Records 815 Broadway New York NY 10003. Reissues of classical vocal 78s.

BELGIAN ILLUSTRIOUS VOICES SERIES Reissues of 78s of Belgian singers—Amiseau, Bovy, Heldy *etc.*

BJR DISCS (USA) Ex-broadcast and pirated opera sets, including Gounod's *Queen of Sheba.* Good boxes and librettos.

CANTILENA Rococo Records *qv.*

CLUB 99 4239 81st Street Elmhurst NY 11373. Reissues of classical vocal 78s.

DISC Orchestral and instrumental music, including Tchaikovsky *Fifth symphony*—RAI/Furtwängler.

EJS (E J Smith NY) 'Golden Age of Opera'. A vast catalogue of off-the-air and archive performances, mainly of opera.

ETERNA Lyrichord Discs Inc 141 Perry St New York NY 10014. Reissues of vocal classical 78s.

WILHELM FURTWANGLER SOCIETY 5 Evrington Lane Leicester. Some reissues of Furtwängler material.

GALLIARD Available from Stainer & Bell, 82 High Road London N2. One LP to date—Warlock songs published by Galliard.

GENESIS RECORDS 225 Santa Monica Boulevard Suite 1107 Santa Monica California 90401. Professionally made recordings of the obscure European nineteenth century romantic repertoire.

IGS Boxed pirated opera sets, including Floyd's *Susanah* and Delius's *Koanga.* These appear to be recorded in the hall and not from broadcasts.

INTERNATIONAL PIANO LIBRARY 215 W 91st Street New York NY 10024. Reissues of historic piano recordings.

IRCC (International Record Collectors Club) The name dates back to 78 days, although a range of LP reissues of classical vocal 78s appeared.

KEYBOARD IMMORTALS Sony Superscope 8150 Vineland Avenue Sun Valley California 91353. Stereo tapes of reproducing pianos.

KLAVIER RECORD CO 5652 Willowcrest Avenue North Hollywood California 91601. Stereo recordings of reproducing pianos. Each record featuring a specific performer.

FRANK MERRICK SOCIETY 29 Gordon Place London W8. LPs of Frank Merrick, specially recorded.

METROPOLITAN MUSEUM OF ART New York. One single-sided LP 'Centennial Fanfares'.

MORGAN DISCS (USA) Ex-broadcast opera sets in excellent sound and superb pressings, housed in fine boxes.

MR (USA) Pirate opera sets. No boxes—the only set seen Hindemith's *Cardillac* (Fisher-Diskeau).

MRF (USA) Ex-broadcast recordings of opera, superlatively produced in boxes with lengthy notes.

MUSICAL HERITAGE SOCIETY 1991 Broadway New York NY. A vast catalogue of unusual classical music.

OASI DISCS Reissues of classical vocal 78s.

OJI/OJAI Reissues of classical vocal 78s.

OLYMPUS Classical vocal reissues of 78s.

ONSLOW RECORDS 61 Kingswood Road London SW2. Records of 'art-song' performances of folk songs, and folk-arrangements.

OPERA VIVA Ex-broadcast opera sets. (The only set seen is Callas/ Serefin performance of *Norma* 29/6/1955).

OPUS Cleveland Ohio. Ex-broadcast orchestral music and some reissues of 78s.

PARNASSUS RECORDS PO Box 281 Phoenicia NY 12464. Reissues mainly of classical orchestral and instrumental music.

PEARL RECORDS 56 Hopwood Gardens Tunbridge Wells Kent. Reissues of instrumental and orchestral classical 78s, particularly acoustic recordings with Elgar conducting. Also issue amateur performances of rarely played works.

PENZANCE Rare opera sets. Ex-broadcast and archive opera sets; very fine pressings.

PERENNIAL RECORDS PO Box 437 New York NY 10023. Reissues of a variety of historic classical recordings.

PHORION Los Angeles. Orchestral music from 'pirate' tapes. Furt-wängler's *Piano Concerto* and a Korngold LP.

PREISER Vienna. Lebendige Vergangenheit and Court Opera Classics. Reissues of classical vocal 78s. Also on Preiser, a few ex-broadcast operas.

RARE RECORDED EDITION 54 Lymington Road London NW6. Amateur performances of rare works, also piano records by Merrick and de Lara.

RARITAS Ex-broadcast opera sets in beautiful pressings.

ROCOCO RECORDS LTD PO Box 175 Station 'K' Toronto 12 Ontario Canada. Reissues of classical vocal and orchestral 78s.

RUBINI RECORDS Woodbridge Record Shop 4a Cumberland Square Woodbridge Suffolk. Reissues of classical vocal 78s.

SCALA Everest Records 10920 Wilshire Boulevard Suite 410 Los Angeles California 90024. Reissues of classical vocal 78s.

SJG DISCS Woodbridge Record Shop. See Rubini above. A few early discs issued under this name.

SJS Pirate issues of instrumental music. Only disc seen—Bain/Saltpeter/Preede in Schubert and Brahms.

SOCIETY FOR THE PRESERVATION OF THE AMERICAN MUSICAL HERITAGE PO Box 4244 Grand Central Station New York NY 10017. Professionally made recordings of American music of the eighteenth, nineteenth and early twentieth centuries.

TAP (Top Artist Platters) Reissues of vocal classical 78s.

TIMA CLUB Numbered limited editions of reissued vocal classic 78s.

TOSCANINI SOCIETY 812 Dumas Avenue Dumas Texas 72029. LPs of Toscanini performances from air checks and unissued 78s.

UNIQUE OPERA RECORDINGS CORPORATION New name for EJS *qv*.

UNIVERSITY OF ILLINOIS RECORDS University of Illinois, Urbana, Illinois.

BRUNO WALTER SOCIETY 71 School Street Waltham Massachusetts 02184. Ex-broadcast performances by Walter and other conductors. Also reissues of commercial 78s and non-commercial Szigeti material.

WESTERN SOUND ARCHIVE 1298 Los Olivos Avenue Los Osos California 93401. Wide collection of orchestral archive recordings on tape. Comprehensive catalogue issued.

XIV

JOURNALS, REVIEW SOURCES AND SERIES

In addition to the usual discographical review sources (which are discussed on page 114) there are a number of journals that contribute to the discographer's task and yet are not part of the regular periodical press of the record industry. There are three main groups of such items: journal literature outside music, which nevertheless review selectively, notable examples being newspapers; secondly, the musical press which is not primarily concerned with records yet gives them good coverage; finally small circulation and mimeographed publications devoted to the history of the gramophone, to advertising second-hand records for sale, and dealing with very specific collecting topics.

GENERAL NON-MUSICAL PRESS

In the UK the most important source for record reviews is the *Financial times* which very often gives superb long and detailed reviews of records but is of course extremely selective; the *Daily telegraph, Guardian* and *Times* are also good though rarely at such length. The Sunday newspapers also have record reviews, though not so frequently—but the *Sunday times, Observer* and *Sunday telegraph* are all worth scanning. Of the weeklies, the *Listener* is brief, but occasionally deals with more unusual material.

GENERAL MUSICAL PRESS

The two major monthly British musical journals, the *Musical times* and *Music and musicians*, both have good coverage of records, and the more important new issues get reviewed, often at considerable length. The more specialist press also reviews, and such journals as *Early music, The organ yearbook* and *English church music* produce more specialised reviews often of more than local interest.

In this context a journal such as *Le grand baton*, journal of the Sir Thomas Beecham Society, and other similar society journals are often highly specialised and unique sources of information.

However, it is not only with reviews that such journals are of value, but with retrospective discographical surveys of specific topics. This is a feature of *Opera,* and is guaranteed to be authoritative. These journals are also of value in just listing such material. *Composer* used to perform a valuable service to all interested in contemporary British music, by listing all the recordings that had been issued, on a regular basis. A similar function is now carried out by a regular annual column in the journal.

As one may see, discography is relevant to most areas of research today, and it is probable that there will be some sort of coverage in the journal literature of any subject.

In the USA, the *Musical quarterly* and the *Journal of the American musicological society* both publish authoritative scholarly reviews. However, the American musical scene is perhaps most valuable for the indexes to reviews that appear in *Notes* and as separate publications in the *Polart index* and *Record and tape reviews index*. Popular reviews are now covered for the first time in Armitage and Dean's *Annual index to popular music record reviews* 1972 (Metuchen NJ, Scarecrow Press, 1973). Record reviews are also covered in the *Music index*.

Finally, on the subject of ' pirate ' records, the recently established journal *The musical newsletter* (Box 250 Lennox Hill Station, New York 10021), regularly publishes comparative critical reviews (see illus VI) of such material (a practice also followed by the one independent regular reviewing journal, the *American record guide*).

LITTLE MAGAZINES
Amateurs produce a number of invaluable journals in the field of discography. These are usually published as a hobby, sometimes as an aid to selling second hand records. Sometimes whole journals are devoted to advertisements, or the editorial matter is a front to the true purpose of carrying lists of material available. These magazines are poorly documented and usually short-lived, but can provide invaluable sources, particularly when they contain discographies. They are listed below under three headings: Jazz; Folk, Country and Western and Pop; and ' Serious ' Music.

JAZZ
Jazz bazaar   Hohenweg 10
                   5461 Rotterheide
                   Germany

Jazz report   357 Leighton Drive   *or* 4 Hillcrest Gardens
                  Ventura   London NW2
                  California 93001
                  USA
Matrix: jazz record research, incorporating *The discophile*
                  115 Duke Road
                  London W4
Vintage jazz mart
                  4 Hillcrest Gardens
                  London NW2

FOLK, COUNTRY & WESTERN, AND POPULAR MUSIC
    Collecta vintage record magazine
                  64 Bucknall's Drive
                  Watford
                  Herts
    Country and western review; previously *Country and western record
    review* and *Country and western express*
                  68 Golden House
                  Great Pulteney St
                  London W1
    Country news and views
                  43 May Road
                  Lowestoft
                  Suffolk
    International film collector [specialises in soundtrack recordings]
                  31 Chapel Road
                  Worthing
                  Sussex
    Memory lane 18 Ambleside Close
                  Seaton Delaval
                  Whitley Bay
                  Northumberland
    Recorded folk music [a review of British and foreign folk music]
                  Collets Holdings
    RSVP   5 Tollet Street
                  London E1

SERIOUS MUSIC (see also p 102-103)
Le grand baton
> 664 South Irena Avenue
> Redondo Beach
> California 90277
> USA

Record advertiser
> 10 Fernhill Road
> Olton
> Solihull
> Warwicks

78RPM   [No longer published, appeared during 1968-1969]

MISCELLANEOUS
Hill and dale news
> 19 Glendale Road
> Southbourne
> Bournemouth
> Hants

The talking machine review
> 19 Glendale Road
> Southbourne
> Bournemouth
> Hants

REVIEW SOURCES : UNITED KINGDOM

In 1958 Clough and Cuming published a list of some of the gramophone review journals that flourish outside the USA (*Notes*, September 1958 p 537-558). This covered some thirty two titles in fifteen countries including Great Britain. More recently, the *Phonographic bulletin* has also published a useful list. The following concentrates on the current scene in the UK and USA.

With the demise of *Audio record review,* there are left in the UK two long established reviewing journals for records, *The Gramophone* which has recently celebrated fifty years of continuous reviewing, and *Records and recording* which complements *The Gramophone* by reason of its slightly glossier presentation, and long feature articles. Two more recently launched journals should also be noted, firstly *Hi Fi news and record review* which is quickly making a unique niche for itself by reason of its bright style and varied features. However, it has not yet achieved the sheer coverage of *The Gramophone,* or even *Records and recording,* but its commentary is lively and interesting. *Audio,* the latest journal to present a glossy and popular style, is of little value for detailed or authoritative assessments as yet, and again has not achieved the sheer coverage of the older journals.

The Gramophone is always the journal to use when there is a matter of fact to be elucidated—identification of an unusual work, or a reissued 78. If background or general commentary is important then *Records and recording* is often of great value too—particularly if the item in question happens to be the subject of a full length feature. The latter also publishes discographies, something *The Gramophone* rarely does these days.

Of the remaining journals, *EMG monthly letter* is a monthly supplement to *The art of record buying,* the select annual list of recommended records issued by the London record shop, EMG. Another record shop, Henry Stave, is responsible for the other journal which is of unique character, in that it follows its own reviews with an attempt at evaluating what the rest of the journal literature thought of the record in question. Thus *Concensus and review* is a valuable short cut to record evaluation. It ceased publication for a short time early in the 1970s, but is active again in 1973.

REVIEW SOURCES: UNITED STATES

The two major American reviewing journals are *Hi-fi stereo review,* and *High fidelity.* The only regular independent journal is the *American record guide.* However, as far as reviews are concerned the regular feature in *Notes,* 'Index to record reviews', is an invaluable guide to sources of reviews of American issues, and a useful guide to British/ American issues as they are reviewed. Journals in both countries are indexed and the list is thereby made a useful by-product in that it becomes a consolidated list of all issues that have appeared.

NEW ISSUES

United Kingdom

To obtain a complete list of the new issues announced each month by the major record companies is comparatively easy, for in the last resort one can always consult their promotion literature, although one should remember that because a record is scheduled for release is no guarantee of its appearance. However, a major problem is that of the small or even non-commercial enterprises and in this circumstance it is probably best to rely on their literature than hope to find all the records issued in the commercially published lists.

As far as commercially published lists of records are concerned, *The Gramophone* lists are probably the major tools both for the collector and the trade in the UK, but it should be remembered that they are not comprehensive and the popular catalogue in particular cannot be relied on for covering the field. Of course, the *Classical catalogue* is a different matter and is all but comprehensive. New releases are not listed separately from the main listing each time there is a new edition of the catalogue published, and so *The Gramophone* magazine is the only guide from this source to the new records each month.

In the journal literature in the UK, the only comprehensive listing of new issues is the feature ' New issues ' which appears at the front of each issue of *Records and recording* which lists them all company by company). The monthly publication *The new records* (20 East Hill, St Austell, Cornwall) fills a similar role, and has the advantage of being solely devoted to its purpose, and is therefore small and easily handled, and can be used for marking-up. The arrangement by company appears to be common in all such listings in the UK.

The fact that pop records are seldom reviewed in the more august journals is largely owing to the specialised methods used to promote them, as they are, from a manufacturer's viewpoint, a very ephemeral product. *The new singles,* by the same publisher as *The new records,* and the weekly issues of the *Melody maker* are invaluable guides to new releases in the pop field. But because of the lack of retrospective indexing—even in indexing journals—both are of limited use as retrospective tools.

The new media of cassettes and cartridges are catered for by a new journal under that title promoted by *The Gramophone* and by a monthly list of new issues rather similar to *The new records* called *The new cassettes and cartridges,* which is published by the same firm. In terms of retrospective specialist listings, the *Record mirror/ Music week* bi-annual publication *The tape guide* is becoming increasingly valuable, particularly for its coverage of the popular field.

NEW ISSUES
United States
The single widely used list of new issues in the USA is the ' New listings ' section that now appears in the front of each month's issue

of *Schwann*. However, there are a number of trade-orientated services listing new issues. Probably the most widely used new issue guides are the *Weekly new release reporter* and the *Monthly popular guide*. Others include the more expensive loose-leaf *Phonolog* which is updated three times a week and the twice-weekly *One-spot numerical index* which lists all new records by number.

With the bringing of records within the orbit of copyright legislation in 1972 in the USA, the Library of Congress accession lists should assume ever increasing importance to those attempting comprehensive coverage, albeit retrospectively.

JOURNALS

Very few journals publish discographies as an end in themselves. In England the major outlet is the quarterly *Recorded sound*. In addition to this the *Record collector* is an important source for discographies devoted to singers. Until recently, short discographies were often appended to feature articles that appeared in *Audio record review*, and with the demise of that journal its style in this respect has passed to the magazine *Hi fi news and record review*.

In the ' serious ' music field, there have grown two journals of major discographical interest in the USA. Though neither are devoted primarily to discographers, they publish frequent discographies. Probably the more important of the two is the *Journal of the Association of Recorded Sound Collections*, while less official but no less enthusiastic is the *International piano library bulletin* of New York.

However, another important outlet for such compilations as we have seen is the less formal, amateur production, often from typescript, that achieves a limited but enthusiastic audience. The short-lived but authentic doyen of this movement was *78RPM*, which only lasted for eight issues, and has been followed by the *Record advertiser*. A more recently founded publication is *Antique records* which from its first issues looks as if it will become an important voice in the discographical field.

Attention should also be given to the similar publications issued by various composer-societies—Bax Society, Spohr Society, Delius Society, Furtwängler Society, Berlioz Society, Liszt Society, *etc*— and these may well be suitable outlets for the appropriate compilation. Indeed, it is just such a society in the USA that provides the major outlet for discographies of conductors—*Le grand baton*, journal of the Sir Thomas Beecham Society. (See p 114.)

JOURNALS PUBLISHING DISCOGRAPHIES

Antique records (Half-yearly) Carradale, 29 Embercourt Road, Thames Ditton, Surrey.

Hi fi news and record review (Monthly) Link House, Dingwall Ave., Croydon.

Record advertiser (Bi-monthly) 10 Fernhill Road, Olton, Solihull, Warwicks.

Record collector (A monthly magazine for collectors of recorded vocal art) 17 St Nicholas Street, Ipswich, Suffolk.

Recorded sound (Quarterly journals of the BIRS 29 Exhibition Road, London SW7).

SERIES

1. Voices of the past series, vocal recordings 1898-1925, published by the Oakwood Press Tandridge Lane Lingfield Surrey.
Vol 1 *The English catalogues*, by John R Bennett.

part 1 : HMV nos	151 to 2-2733 1956
2	2-2735 to 3284 1957
3	3285 to 04807; miscellaneous B298-B459 1957
4	B460-B2098, C419-C770 1957
5	C772-C1216, E3-E398, D1-D1024 1957

Index to artists 1957

reissued in one volume : *HMV English catalogue*, 1957.

Vol 2 *HMV Italian catalogues* by John R Bennett. A catalogue of vocal recordings from the Italian catalogue of the Gramophone Co, Ltd, 1899-1900, The Gramophone Co (Italy) Ltd, 1899-1909, The Gramophone Co, Ltd, 1909, Compagnia Italiana dei Grammofono 1909-1912, Societa Nazionale del Grammofono 1910-1925 1958.

Vol 3 *Dischi fonotipia* by John R Bennett. Republication in one volume of : Bennett, John R *Dischi fonotipia*, Ipswich, The Record Collector Shop 1953 (Limited edition of 1000 copies); Supplement to *Dischi fonotipia* 1958.

Vol 4 *The International Red Label catalogue* by John R Bennett *and* Eric Hughes. Book 1 HMV DB 12 inch series 1961.

Vol 5 *HMV Black Label catalogue* (D & E Series) by Michael Smith 1972.

Vol 6 *The International Red Label catalogue* by John R Bennett *and* Eric Hughes. Book 2 HMV DA series 1963.

Vol 7 A Catalogue of vocal recordings from the 1898-1925 *German catalogues* of the Gramophone Company Ltd, Deutsche Grammophon A-G, by John R Bennett *and* Wilhelm Wimmer, 1967.

Vol 8 *The Columbia catalogue English celebrity issues* by Michael Smith *and* Ian Cosens 1972.

Vol 9 A catalogue of vocal records from the 1898-1925 *HMV French catalogues* of the Gramophone Company Ltd, Compagnie Française du Gramophone nd [1973].

2. J F Weber Utica New York Discography series 1970-. Titles include: *Loewe, Franz, Mahler, Bruckner, Schubert's lieder, Mendelssohn's vocal music.*

3. Keystone Books in Music. Philadelphia, Lippincott. Annotated lists of currently available recordings in a given field:

Briggs, John: *The collector's Tchaikovsky Modern and the Five* 1959

Briggs, John: *The collector's Beethoven* 1962.

Broder, Nathan: *The collector's Bach* 1958

Burke, C G: *The collector's Haydn* 1959

Cohn, Arthur: *The collector's twentieth-century music in the western hemisphere* [American music] 1961

Schonberg, Harold C: *The collector's Chopin and Schumann* 1959

4. Nationaldiskoteket series of discographies (Copenhagen):

Bjerre, C Fabricius-: *Carl Nielsen: a discography* [1965] 2nd ed. 1968.

Hansen, Hans: *Lauritz Melchior: a discography* 1965 2nd ed. 1972

Rosenberg, Herbert: *Aksel Schiøtz: a discography* 1966

Rosenberg, Herbert: *The Danish His Master's Voice DA and DB series 1950-1952* 1965

Olsen, Henning Smidth: *Wilhelm Furtwängler: a discography* 1970

Edition Balzer: *A Danish history of music in sound* 1966

Jussi Bjoerling: a record list 1969.

5. Swedish National Phonotheque discographies:

No 9 Resia by Karleric Liliedahl 1969

10 Dacapo by Karleric Liliedahl 1969

11 Sonora V: 2000/3000 series Vol 1 by Björn England nd

501 Ernst Rolf by Karleric Liliedahl 1970

502 Ulla Billquist by Gunnar Brederick 1970
[E5000, E6000, E9000, K9500 series]
Sonora IV by Björn England 1968.
Nationaldiskoteket: Nominalkatalog över Dokumentärmaterial
1962 *supp* 1 1963; *supp* 2 1965.
6. Archives of recorded music. Archives de la musique enregistrée.
Paris, UNESCO, 1949-.
Series A Western Music vol 1: L'oeuvre de Frédéric Chopin. Paris,
Edition de la Revue Disques, 1949.
Series B Oriental Music vol 1: Catalogue of recorded classical and
traditional Indian music by A Daniélou. Paris, UNESCO, 1952.
Series C Ethnographical and folk music vol 1: Collection phonothèque nationale. Paris, UNESCO 1952.
vol. 2: Collection Musée de l'Homme. Paris, UNESCO 1952.
vol. 3: Katalog der europäischen Volksmusik im Schallarchiv des
Institutes für Musikforschung, Regensburg, edited by Felix
Hoerburger. Regensburg, Bosse 1952.
vol 4: International catalogue of recorded folk music, edited by
Norman Fraser. OUP, 1954.
7. *Stereo record guide.* Blackpool, Long playing record library, vols
1-8. See page 89.

XV

SELECT LIST OF DISCOGRAPHIES

Although the major flood of discographies started after the second world war, record catalogues as such have been appearing since the end of the first world war. Kurtz Myers[96] has cited the 'phonobretto . . . the indispensable companion of the phonograph, and faithful interpreter of above seven hundred songs and spoken phonograph selections' which appeared in 1919, as the earliest known discography. Of course, manufacturers' and retailers' catalogues go back to the earliest years of the present century.

As far as classical or 'serious' music recordings are concerned, a number of bibliographic guides are available, and these are discussed in my bibliography entitled *Discographies,* published by Triad Press, 1973.

Discographies are also invaluable tools in other fields, not only musical. These include wildlife recordings, documentary, ethnic and folk material, while outside the field of 'serious' music, jazz, folk, pop and entertainment music discographies need to be fully documented. Rust's *The complete entertainment discography* (New Rochelle, NY, Arlington House, 1973) which covers minstrel and vaudeville entertainers, film stars and radio personalities, exemplifies the sheer range possible in sound material.

WILDLIFE DISCOGRAPHIES

A good number of discographies of wildlife recordings, particularly of birdsong, have been compiled. These are not only concerned with the surprisingly large number of commercially issued recordings of wildlife sounds, but also with archival and privately owned materials.

The 'Wildlife special issue' of *Recorded sound* (April 1969) is a major source for anyone wishing to study the discography of wildlife sounds. In the field of birdsounds, mention might also be made of the BBC Further Education Department (Radio) who have issued a free information sheet (ref 03/FE/RJ), of great value in dealing with birdsong, and birdsong recordings.

Most of the following have been compiled by the same person,

5*

Jeffery Boswall of the BBC Natural History Unit, and therefore the compilation methods reflect his personal approach to the problem.

The *Bio-acoustics bulletin*, cited in a number of items, is published by Cornell University, Laboratory of Ornithology, Ithaca, New York, and is available from the British Lending Library in the United Kingdom.

BBC: *Handlist of natural history recordings in the BBC Sound Archives*. Third edition 1961. Bristol, BBC Natural History Unit.

BBC: *Some bird recordings available on commercial gramophone records*. BBC, Further Education Department, Information Sheet, 1970.

Boswall, Jeffery: 'A British discography of wildlife sound'. *Recorded sound* April 1969, p 463-465.

Boswall, Jeffery: 'A catalogue of tape and gramophone records of Australian region bird sound'. *The emu, 65*, Part 1, August 1965, p 65-74.

Boswall, Jeffery *and* Prytherch, R J: 'A discography of birds sounds from the Antarctic zoogeographical region'. *Polar record*, XIV, no 92, May 1969, p 603-612.

Boswall, Jeffery *and* North, Myles: 'A discography of bird sound from the Ethiopian zoogeographical region'. *Ibis* 109, 1967, p 521-533.

Boswall, Jeffery: 'A discography of Palearctic amphibian sound recordings'. *British journal of herpetology* 3, no 11, 1966, p 286-289.

Boswall, Jeffery: 'A discography of palearctic bird sound recordings'. *British birds* 57, 1964. Special supplement. Published by H F & G Witherby Ltd, London EC4.

Boswall, Jeffery: 'New Palearctic bird sound recordings in 1964-65'. *British birds* 59, January 1966, p 27-37.

Boswall, Jeffery: 'New Palearctic bird sound recordings in 1966-67'. *British birds* 62, February 1969, p 49-65.

Boswall, Jeffery: 'New Palearctic bird sound recordings during 1968'. *British birds* 62, July 1969, p 271-281.

Boswall, Jeffery: 'A discography of Palearctic insect sound recording'. *Entomologists record* 78, no 9, 1966, p 202-206.

Boswall, Jeffery: 'A discography of Palearctic mammal sound recording'. *Recorded sound* April/July 1966, p 88-89.

Boswall, Jeffery: 'A discography of wildlife sound'. *SFTA journal* 33/33, 1968, p 84.

Boswall, Jeffery: [List of all commercial records of insects]. *Recorded sound* April 1969, p 457.

Boswall, Jeffery: 'Recording the voices of captive birds'. *The avicultural magazine*, May-June, 1963, p 121-127.

Boswall, Jeffery: *Voice recordings of the anatidiae*. Twelfth Annual Report of the Wildfowl Trust 1961, p 147-150.

Boswall, Jeffery: 'A world catalogue of gramophone records of bird voice'. *Bio-acoustics bulletin* 1 (2) p 1-12.

Boswall, Jeffery: Amendments and additions to 'A world catalogue of gramophone records of bird voice', October/December 1962. *Bio-acoustics bulletin* 2 (3 & 4) p 25-29.

Boswall, Jeffery: Further amendments and additions to 'A world catalogue of gramophone records of bird voice, and a geographical index'. *Bio-acoustics bulletin* 4 (1), January/March 1964, p 6-10.

Robinson, F N: *Catalogue of recorded bird calls*. Canberra, Commonwealth Scientific and Industrial Research Organisation. Division of Wildlife Research, 1970.

JAZZ DISCOGRAPHIES

There have not been many attempts at compiling bibliographies of discographies in the jazz field. Probably the most practicable is the bibliography in Langridge's *Your jazz collection* (Bingley, 1970) which provides a good basic introduction to the field (p 53-55). Otherwise, *Jazz studies* vol 2 No 3 (The British Institute of Jazz Studies) includes a long bibliography of discographies of specific jazz performers, while the short section 'Further reading' in R W W Dixon's *Recording the blues* (Studio Vista, 1970) (p 108) gives a useful guide in a very specific subject area. Anderson's *Helpful hints* (Baraboo, Wisconsin, Andoll, 1957) is also worth knowing about. Finally, although only containing a very short guide to discographies of jazz, the chapter entitled 'Collecting jazz records' which Alexander Ross contributed to Semeonoff's *Record collecting*,[16] is recommendable on a broader level as a good, practical, but superficial introduction to the subject.

The following select discography has been arranged in alphabetical order, but has been kept short enough for it to be scanned quickly. All the publications mentioned above will supplement it in a practical way.

Carey, Dave *and* McCarthy, Albert J: [Jazz Directory] *The directory of recorded jazz and swing music*. Vols 1-4 (A-I) 1950-51 Fordingbridge Hants.

Cherrington, George *and* Knight, Brian: *Jazz catalogue—a complete discography.* Jazz journal, 1964.

Decca Record Company: *Jazz on 78s, 1954. Jazz on Lps,* revised 1956.

Delaunay, Charles: *New hot discography.* NY, Critterion 1948.

Dixon, Robert W W *and* Godrich, John: *Recording the blues.* Studio Vista, 1970.

Fox, Charles: Discography. In *His jazz in perspective.* BBC, 1969.

Godrich, John *and* Dixon, Robert M W: *Blues and gospel records 1902-1942.* Revised edition 1969. Storyville Publications 63 Oxford Road London E17.

Harris, Rex *and* Rust, Brian: *Recorded jazz: a critical guide.* Penguin, 1958.

Jepson, J G: *Jazz records.* Denmark, Knudsen, 1963 *8 vols.*

Lange, Horst: *Die deutsche 78er-Discographie der Jazz-und-Hot-Dance-Musik 1903-58.* Berlin, Colloquium Verlag, 1966.

Ledbitter, Mike *and* Slaven, Neil: *Blues records: January 1943 to December 1966.* Hanover Books (NY, Oak Publications), 1968.

McCarthy, Albert *and others*: *Jazz on record: a critical guide to the first 50 years, 1917-67.* Hanover Books (NY, Oak Publications), 1968.

Massaglia, Luciano *and others*: *Duke Ellington's story on records.* Milan, Musica Jazz vol 2 (1932-1938) 1966; vol 3 (1939-1942) 1967; vol 4 (1953-1944) 1968; vol 5 (1945) 1968.

Panassie, Hugues: *Hugues Panassie discusses 144 hot jazz Bluebird and Victor records.* Camden, NJ, RCA, 1939.

Panassie, Hugues: *Discographie critique des meilleurs disques de jazz.* Geneva, Crasset, 1948.

Ramsey, Frederic: *A guide to longplay jazz records.* NY, Long Player Publications, 1954.

Rust, Brian: *Jazz records 1897-.* Second edition, Arlington House, 1969.

Rust, Brian: *Negro blues and gospel records.* Hatch End, Middlesex, Brian Rust, 1965.

Smith, C E *and others*: *The Jazz record book.* NY, Smith & Durrell, 1942.

Wilson, John S: *The collectors' jazz: traditional and swing.* Philadelphia, Lippincott, 1958.

Wilson, John S: *The collectors' jazz: modern and progressive.* Philadelphia, Lippincott, 1959.

ETHNIC AND FOLK MATERIALS

This brief survey of the very large subject of ethnomusicology is meant to indicate the sort of material that may be found, and the scope of the subject. Not only the in-situ recordings of primitive musical cultures are involved, but the question of speech recordings of such cultures, and the larger and more developed one of ' folk music ', and all that term implies, from the still existing traditional song-art of small communities, to the developing one of the song of the industrial community. The merging with jazz, pop music and country and western music, makes a very large potential field.

Those dealing with ethnomusicology for the first time should read the three major general background studies by Kunst (*Ethnomusicology,* The Hague, Martinus Nijhoff, 1969), McAllester (*Readings in ethnomusicology,* New York and London, Johnson Reprint Corp, 1971) and Nettl (*Theory and method in ethnomusicology,* Free Press of Glencoe [Collier-Macmillan], 1964), to obtain a general view of the subject and the importance of discography. The importance of the techniques of field-recordings should not be underestimated, and it is vital that the discographer realises the nature of the material with which he is dealing. In this respect Maud Karpeles' short guide is invaluable (*The collecting of folk music and other ethnomusicological material—a manual for field workers.* The International Folk Music Council and the Royal Anthropological Institute of Great Britain, 1958).

Another good perspective of the whole question of ethnomusicological materials may be gained from the special issue of *Recorded sound* devoted to ' Technical media in the preservation and dissemination of classical and traditional music of the orient and folk music of the orient and occident '. (April/July 1963.)

A general guide to current discographical work in the strictly ethnomusicological field appeared in 1968 by Hickerson and Roberts (*Ethnomusicology* no 1 1968, p 110-139) but there has been little by way of discography of discographies, although a number of comprehensive studies of particular fields.

Three American items in the folk song field should be noted before we pass on to deal with the main matter of this section. Firstly, R M

Lawless's handbook of biography, bibliography and discography entitled *Folksingers and folksong in America* (Snell, Sloan and Pearce, nd [1960]) that stands on the borders of traditional material, and the 'composed' folksong of today. Secondly, typical discographical studies of small areas of the folksong of the industrial society, Green's discographies of American labour union songs and of coal miners' songs as revealed by the LP record ('A discography [LP] of American labour union songs'. *New York folk quarterly* no 3, 1961, p 186-193; *and* 'A discography of American coal miners' songs'. *Labour history* no 1, 1961, p 101-115). Both are revealing of the sort of material that is to be dealt with.

The sort of valuable perspective that a knowledge of ethnomusicological materials gives to all musicians and music historians is shown by Joan Rimmer in her article 'Locally issued records of regional music' (*Bulletin of the BIRS*, Autumn 1959, p 3-5) in which she gives examples of recordings of instruments that give some idea of the development of, for example, Clarinets, or Shawms and Bagpipes.

When dealing with discographies in the field of primitive and strange cultures there is a clear differentiation to be made between material that is preserved in a specific archive (often available in copies to students, in contradistinction to western art music in such archives) and material that has been issued on commercially available discs, although even these are usually available from some specialist label or organisation. Both sorts of material are to be found in the following discographies.

GENERAL

Fraser, Norman *editor: International catalogue of recorded folk music;* with a preface by R Vaughan Williams, and introduced by Maud Karpeles. OUP, 1954 (Archives of recorded music, series C: Ethnographical and folk music vol 4).

Italian State Record Library: *Catalogue of recordings in the Ethnolinguistics-Ethnomusicoloy Archive. Archivio Ethnico Linguistico Musicale: Catalogo dell registrazione. Catalogue of recordings in the Ethnolinguistics-Ethnomusicology Archive of the Italian State Record Library,* Rome: Presidenza del Consiglio dei Ministri, Servizi Informazioni e Proprietà Letteraria Artistica e Scientifica, 1967. (Reviewed in *Recorded sound* vol 68, p 348-349.)

Wachsmann, Klaus P: An international catalogue of published records of folk music. *Bulletin of the BIRS,* Summer and Autumn

1960) (whole double issue). ('This catalogue is supplementary to . . . the *International catalogue of recorded folk music* . . .')

AFRICA

International Library of African Music: *The sound of Africa* [a catalogue of LP records]. Roodepoort, Transvaal, South Africa, 1963.

Merriam, Alan P: *African music on LP: an annotated discography.* Evanston, Northwestern University Press, 1970.

AMERICAS

Shultz, H: 'Some American Indian music on records'. *American record guide.* May 1949, p 259-262; June 1949, p 291-296; Sept 1949, p 7-10.

Archive of American Folksong: *A list of American folksongs currently available on records.* Library of Congress, 1953.

Duran, Gustavo: *Recordings of Latin-American songs and dances.* Pan-American Union, 1950.

ASIA *general*

Crossley-Holland, Peter: 'Oriental music on the gramophone'. *Music and letters* January 1959, p 56-71.

Purcell, W L: 'The music of Asia—a discography'. *American record guide,* September 1959, p 8-11.

Crossley-Holland, Peter: 'International catalogue of records of the folk and classical music of the orient commercially available on 31 December 1962'. *Recorded sound* April/July 1963, p 75-102.

ASIA *India, Pakistan & Tibet*

Daniélou, Alain: *A catalogue of recorded classical and traditional Indian music.* Paris, Unesco, 1952.

Purcell, W L: 'A discography: India, Pakistan and Tibet'. *American record guide,* March 1960, p 568-569.

ASIA *Indonesia, Southeast Asia and the Philippines*

Purcell, W L: 'A discography of Indonesia, Southeast Asia, and the Philippines'. *American record guide,* May 1961, p 707.

ASIA *Japan*

Waterhouse, David: 'Hogaku preserved; a select-list of long playing records . . . of the national music of Japan'. *Recorded sound,* January 1969, p 383-402.

Moyle, A M: 'Australian aboriginal music, a bibliography and discography'. *Canon* 1964 17, no 3, p 39-40.

Australian Institute of Aboriginal Studies: *Catalogue of tape archive.* Canberra. (Nine issues up to April 1972.)

Folk music record archives have been established in many countries, and enquiries directed to these organisations may well be a more profitable way of tracing material within their speciality than by trying to trace a relevant discography. A good directory of such organisations appeared in *Recorded sound* in 1963 (International Folk Music Council: 'International directory of folk music record archives'. *Recorded sound* April/July 1963, p 103-114.)

XVI

BIBLIOGRAPHY

GENERAL

1 Batten, Joe: *The story of sound recording*. Rockliff, 1956.

2 Bryant, E T: *Collecting gramophone records*. Focal Press, 1962.

3 Burns, Richard: 'The legacy of the phonograph'. *Music and musicians*, March 1973, p 22-27.

4 Chew, V K: *Talking machines 1877-1914*. HMSO, 1967.

5 Chambers, J Bescoby-: *Archives of sound*. Lingfield, Oakwood Press, nd [196?].

6 Crabbe, John: *Hi fi in the home*. Blandford, 3rd ed 1972.

7 de Nys, Carl: *La discothèque idéale*. Paris: Editions Universitaires, 1960.

8 Edney, Eric: 'The matrix mystery'. *Record collector*, February 1963, p 14-18.

9 Gelatt, Roland: *The fabulous phonograph*. Cassell; NY, Lippincott, 1956.

10 Hurst, P G: *The golden age recorded*. Lingfield, Oakwood Press, 2nd ed 1963.

11 Kellog, Peter Paul: 'Problems of storing natural sounds on tape'. *Bio-acoustics bulletin*, January-March 1962, p 2-4.

12 Martin, James: *The £sd of record collecting*. Lingfield, Oakwood Press, 1956.

13 Moir, James: *High quality sound reproduction*. Chapman and Hall, 1958.

14 Pickett, A G *and* Lemcoe, M M: *Preservation and storage of sound recordings*. Washington, Library of Congress, 1959.

15 Political and Economic Planning: 'The gramophone record: industry and art'. *Planning*, November 5 1951.

16 Semeonoff, Boris: *Record collecting*, Lingfield, Oakwood Press, 1949; 2nd ed 1951.

17 Strutt, Mary (compiler): *Fifty years of the BBC—a select list of books*. Westminster City Libraries, 1972.

18 Tremaine, Howard M: *The audio cyclopedia*. Indianapolis, Howard W Sams & Co, nd [1960].

19 Watts, Agnes: *Cecil E Watts: pioneer of direct disc recording.* Privately published, 1972.

20 Wimbush, Roger: *The gramophone jubilee book.* Gramophone Publications, 1973.

21 Young, J Lewis: *Edison and his phonograph* (1890). Bournemouth, The Talking Machine Review, nd [196?]. Facsimile reprint.

SOUND ARCHIVES

Directories

22 'Recensement international provisoire des phonothèques'. *Fontes artis musicae,* 1959, p 68-82.

23 Assocation for Recorded Sound Collections: *A preliminary directory of sound recording collections in the United States and Canada.* NY, New York Public Library, 1967.

24 Pop, Sever *and others: Instituts de phonothéque et archivs phonographiques.* Louvain, Commission d'Enquéte Linguistique, 1956.

25 Tainsh, Karin B: 'Radioföretagens ljurdarkiv'. *Biblioteksbladet* 45, 1, 1960, p 21-30.

Individual institutions

26 (Berlin Phonogramm-Archiv) Reinhard, Kurt: *Türkische musik* [in the Berlin Phonogramm-Archiv], Berlin, Museum für Völkerkinde, 1962.

27 (BIRS) Shawe-Taylor, D: 'The British Institute of Recorded Sound'. *Adult education* 28, no 3, 1955, p 189-194.

28 (BIRS) Saul, P: 'The British Institute of Recorded Sound'. *Fontis artis musicae,* no 2, 1956, p 171-173.

29 (French National Archive) Copyright Society of the USA: *The French National Archive of recording—twenty years of evolution 1940-1960.* (Summary translated by Evelyn Dunne . . . from 'La Phonothéque Nationale, vingt ans d'evolution, 1940-1960, by Roger Decollogue.) Copyright Society of the USA, 1961.

30 (German Radio) Pauli, F W: 'Das lautarchiv des deutschen rundfunks'. *BIRS bulletin,* Spring 1957, p 17-18.

31 (Indiana University) List, G: 'The Indiana University archives of folk and primitive music'. *BIRS bulletin,* no 15/16 1960 p 3-7.

32 (Italian State Sound Archive) Saffi, Count: 'The Italian State Record Library [Discoteca de Stato]'. *BIRS bulletin,* Summer 1956, p 8-11.

33 (Italian State Sound Archive) Discoteca di Stato; Archivio Ethnico Linguistico Musicale: *Catalogo delle registrazione.* Rome, 1967.

34 (Mexico) Soiess, Lincoln *and* Stanford, Thomas: *An introduction to certain Mexican musical archives.* Detroit, Information Coordinators, 1969.

35 (New York) Miller, P L: 'The record archive in the New York Public Library'. *BIRS bulletin,* Summer 1957, p 20-22.

RECORDINGS IN LIBRARIES
36 Amesbury, Dorothy: 'Phonograph records in the library'. *Library journal* 62 June 1 1937, p 453-454.

37 *The audio tape collection.* Salem, Ohio, Dale E Shaffer, 1973.

38 Colby, E E: 'Sound scholarship'. *Library trends,* July 1972, p 7-28.

39 Doebler, Paul: 'Audio tapes seek a place in bookstores, libraries'. *Publishers weekly,* February 19 1973, p 65-68.

40 *Library journal* May 1 1963, p 1809-1840 and October 15 1963, p 3783-3803. (Issues concerning recordings in relation to libraries.)

41 Pearson, Mary D: *Recordings in the public library.* Chicago, American Library Association, 1963.

42 'Picking the pops: one: a minute from 800,000'. *Storage handling distribution,* September 1966, p 41-42.

43 Skallerup, H R: 'Phonograph records in serials'. *Library resources and technical services,* Spring 1963, p 216-218.

RECORD LIBRARIES
44 Colby, E E: 'Sound recordings in the music library'. *Library trends,* April 1960, p 556-565.

45 Currall, Henry F J (editor): *Gramophone record libraries—their organisation and practice.* Crosby Lockwood, 2nd edition 1970. (Includes: *Select bibliography of gramophone record librarianship,* by Miriam H. Miller.)

46 International Association of Music Libraries: *Phonograph record libraries.* Hamden, Connecticut, Archon Books, 1963.

47 Morgan, J L: Music scores and recorded music. (The scope for automatic data processing in the British Library; supporting paper T) Boston Spa, Yorkshire, National Lending Library, 1971. (Published in microfiche format only.)

48 Rosen, Ida *and others*: 'Report of the Education and Standards Committee' [of the Association for Recorded Sound Collections]. *Journal of the ARSC*, Summer/Fall 1968, p 4-47.

49 Stevenson, Gordon (editor): 'Trends in archival and reference collections of recorded sound'. *Library trends*, July 1972 (whole issue).

ASPECTS OF LIBRARIANSHIP FOR THE DISCOGRAPHER
General

50 Arms, William Y *and* Caroline R: *Access to union catalogues maintained by computer*. National Central Library, 1972.

51 Bradley, Carol J (editor): *Manual of music librarianship*. Ann Arbor, Michigan, Music Library Association, 1966.

52 Education and Science, Department of: *The scope of automatic data processing in the British Library*. 2 vols HMSO, 1972. (Recorded music, paras. 490-496.)

53 Foskett, A C: *A guide to personal indexes*. Clive Bingley, 2nd edition 1970.

54 Hunnisett, Roy Frank: *Indexing for editors*. British Records Association, 1972. (Archives and the user, no 2.)

55 Redfern, Brian L: *Organising music in libraries*. Clive Bingley, 1966.

56 Robinson, A M Lewin: *Systematic bibliography*. Clive Bingley, 1966.

57 Spaulding, C Sumner: 'ISBD: its origin, rationale and implication'. *Library journal*, January 15 1973, p 121-123.

58 Swanson, Gerald: 'ISBD: standard or secret?' *Library journal*, January 15 1973, p 124-130.

Standards

59 British Standards Institution: *British standard for bibliographic references*. BS 1929: 1950. BSI, 1951.

60 British Standards Institution: *Specification for bibliographic information interchange format for magnetic tape*. BS 4748:1971. BSI, 1971.

61 British Standards Institution: *Specification for the presentation of bibliographical information in printed music*. BS 4754: 1971. BSI, 1971.

62 Davis, Peter: 'Piracy on the High Cs'. *Music and musicians,* May 1973, p 38-40.

63 Dixon, E I: 'Oral history—a new horizon'. *Library journal,* April 1 1962, p 1363-1365.

64 Saul, Patrick: 'Some problems in the preservation of valuable sounds'. *BIRS, bulletin,* Summer 1959, p 24-30.

65 Shores, Louis: 'The dimensions of oral history'. *Library journal,* March 1 1967, p 979-983.

66 Stevenson, G: 'Echoes of bugle and drum'. *Wilson library bulletin,* February 1963, p 479-482.

CATALOGUING RECORDINGS

Cataloguing codes

67 Miller, Philip L *and others: Interim report of the Committee on the Cataloguing and Filing of Phonograph Records.* Rochester, New York, Music Library Association, 1939.

68 Music Library Association: *Code for cataloging phonograph records.* Music Library Association, 1942.

69 US Library of Congress. Descriptive Cataloging Division: *Rules for descriptive cataloging in the Library of Congress.* Washington DC, Library of Congress, 1949.

70 US Library of Congress. Descriptive Cataloging Division: *Rules for descriptive cataloging in the Library of Congress: phonorecords.* Preliminary edition. Washington DC, Library of Congress, 1952.

71 Bartlett, Merle C: *Manual for phonorecord cataloger.* Berkeley, University of California, 1953.

72 Joint Committee of the Music Library Association and the American Library Association, Division of Cataloging and Classification: *Code for cataloging music and phonorecords.* Chicago, American Library Association, 1958.

73 US Library of Congress. Descriptive Cataloging Division: *Rules for descriptive cataloging in the Library of Congress: phonorecords.* Second preliminary edition. Washington DC, Library of Congress, 1964.

74 American Library Association: *Anglo-American cataloging rules.* Chicago, American Library Association, 1967.

75 *Anglo-American cataloging rules: British text.* The Library Association, 1967.

76 Croghan, Anthony: *A code for cataloguing non book media.* Coburgh Publications, 1972.

Nonbook media

77 Association for Educational Communications and Technology. Cataloging Committee: *Standards for cataloging nonprint materials.* Washington DC, AECT, 1971.

78 Gilbert, Leslie A *and* Wright, Jan W: *Nonbook materials: their bibliographic control—a proposed computer system for the cataloguing of audio-visual materials in the United Kingdom.* National Council for Educational technology, 1971.

79 Grove, Pearse S *and* Clement, Evelyn G: *Bibliographic control of nonprint media.* Chicago, American Library Association, 1972.

80 Lewis, Peter R: ' "Early warning" generic medium designations in multimedia catalogues'. *Library resources and technical services,* Winter 1973, p 66-69.

81 Massonneau, Suzanne: 'Cataloguing nonbook materials—mountain or molehill?'. *Library resources and technical services,* Summer 1972, p 294-314.

82 Phillips, A B: 'Nonbook materials—projects and publications'. *International cataloguing,* April/June 1973, p 6-8.

83 Riddle, Jean *and others: Nonbook materials—the organisation of integrated collections.* Ottawa, Canadian Library Association. Preliminary edition, 1970.

84 Anderson, Sherman: 'Cataloging of "folk music" on records'. *Library resources and technical services,* Winter 1959, p 64-69.

85 Cox, Carl: 'The cataloging of records'. *Library journal,* December 15 1960, p 4523-4525.

86 Cunmon, T: 'The cataloging and classification of phonograph records'. Catholic Library Association Conference, New York 1960, *Proceedings,* p 180-185.

87 Hagen, C B: 'A proposed information retrieval system for sound recordings'. *Special libraries,* April 1965, p 223-228.

88 Ohm, Betty: 'Here's one for the record'. *Illinois libraries,* February 1965, p 120-132. (Deals with the use of *Phonolog* as an analytical index to a library collection.)

89 Oyler, Patricia: *The concept of the main entry as applied to musical phonograph records.* (Unpublished study from the Graduate

School of Librarianship and Information Sciences, University of Pittsburgh) nd [1970].

90 Smith, Margaret Dean-: 'Proposals towards the cataloging of gramophone records in a library of national scope'. *Journal of documentation*, September 1952, p 141-156.

91 Somerville, S A: 'The cataloging of gramophone records'. *The librarian and book world*, July 1959, p 97-99.

DISCOGRAPHY

92 Clough, F F *and* Cuming, G J: 'Discographical difficulties'. Gramophone record review, 1956. (Reprinted from *Fontes artis musicae*, 1956 no 1, p 95-108).

93 Collings, G C (editor): *International discophile*. Fresno, California, International discophile, nd [1956].

94 Cuming, Geoffrey: 'Problems of record cataloguing'. *Recorded sound*, Autumn 1961, p 116-122.

95 Gronow, P: 'Discography as a science'. *Jazz monthly*, August 1968, p 9-12.

96 Myers, K: 'For the collector—discographies help him become an expert'. *New York times*, April 19 1959, p 108.

97 Weaver, William: 'Discography'. [First International Congress of Discography at Treviso.] *Financial times*, July 2 1973, p 3.

APPENDIX

DARRELL'S 'GRAMOPHONE SHOP ENCYCLOPEDIA OF RECORDED MUSIC'

Clough and Cuming acknowledged the importance of Darrell's pioneering work in compiling the first major systematic catalogue of recorded music. There had been predecessors, but Darrell's was the work that all who came after him followed. In view of the general acceptance of the principles he propounded, the preface to the original edition of his encyclopedia is of special interest. Space precludes quoting it in full, but the following extracts will convey the flavour, and the writer hopes, prompt the reader into searching out the original for himself.

R D Darrell (in a letter to the present author) briefly sketched the circumstances of the publication of the first edition of his work as follows: ' In the mid '30s (I started formal work on GSERM in the spring of 1934) we didn't even have the word discography, much less the art/science itself. What I had in mind was the first *catalogue raisonné* of all (I hoped) serious music on records, and my approach was largely intuitive (lacking any models that I knew of). I spent a great deal of time, thought and experiment on the typographical arrangement of my materials, seeking to get the maximum information in a minimum space. You might be interested to learn about a couple of influential factors: I made use of two different types of preparatory exercise as it were: 1—a series of pseudonymous letters in the *Phonograph monthly review* (1926-1932) outlining the principal recorded works of various mostly contemporary composers: 2—more formal surveys, recorded symphonies, recorded chamber music, etc, in the *Music lovers' guide* (1932-1934) (precursor of the present day *American record guide*).'

' PREFACE
The great bulk of the recorded repertory is produced by several international chains of affiliated corporations, but many of its most precious

treasures stem from independent companies or small and often obscure organizations. In the past a disc library could be built up only through the dubious aid of the catalogues and other literature issued by the manufacturers themselves, eked out by dealers' bulletins or circulars and by such magazine and newspaper articles and reviews as might be accessible. And while the industrious accumulation of such material gave an impressive notion of the scope of the repertory and revealed many a notable disc and album-set, the serious student or collector found himself handicapped and confused at every turn. Even the most cursory examination of a batch of record catalogues meets with an immediate problem in the babel of various languages in which they are printed. Few catalogues will be found to contain a complete composers' catalogue (in many there is none at all) and the reader is almost never given any clue to the musical importance of composers whose names are unfamiliar to him. But the greatest deficiency of all catalogues is their failure to provide consistent, systematic identifications of the musical works set on their discs; all of them seem to have been based on the quicksand foundation of the information printed on the labels of the records themselves, information usually provided in haste by the recording artist or his agent and so frequently inadequate or downright inaccurate as to be valueless when they are not definitely misleading. (An album labelled " Symphony in D minor by Franck " is clear enough, since Franck wrote only one such work, but not a " Symphony in D major by Haydn ", for there are over twenty Haydn symphonies in that key. An amateur musician may happen to know that Handel's " Largo " is the aria " Ombra mai fù " from Serse, that the " Air on the G String " is an arrangement of the slow movement of the Bach Orchestral Suite No. 3 in D major, but he is less likely to know that the Bach " Arioso ", Prelude to Cantata No. 156, and the Sinfonie to the Cantata " Ich steh' mit einem Fuss im Grabe " are one and the same work, or that Menuhin's recordings of the Unaccompanied Violin Sonata No. 3 and the Unaccompanied Violin Sonata No. 5 of Bach contain exactly the same music. And, without hearing the discs themselves, how is anyone to know whether two records of a Mozart " Minuet ", a Vivaldi " Adagio ", or a Scarlatti " Sonatina ", are the same or two entirely different pieces?

'And such random examples of labelling and cataloguing annoyances are elementary compared with the hit or miss methods of listing operatic arias; sometimes by the first words of the recitative, sometimes by the first words of the aria, often by the words of a later section of the area, merely by the name of the character who sings it, or even by some descriptive title. No recording company sticks to a consistent plan and for final madness any one of these titles may appear in any one of a dozen languages) . . .

'No attempt has been made to include dance music, popular songs, encore pieces, and such ephemerae, and while the leading composers of operettas and so-called light music are represented, attention is primarily focused on the works of "serious" composers; not only the familiar names of the classical and romantic schools, but also every significant figure of our own day whose work is exemplified on discs. And—believing that the tragedy of our musical culture is its pitifully circumscribed range of interest, its failure to pay more than lip service to catholicity—the Compiler has devoted particular attention to the giants of the great polyphonic era that flourished before Bach, as alien to contemporary concert-goers as the Babylonian and Mayan civilizations, but resurrected by our once derided mechanistic contraption to restore a lost heritage of the purest and richest tonal tradition the world has ever known.

' This is a work dedicated to creative rather than executive artists, to composers rather than performers (recorded repertories of the latter may be traced without difficulty in the catalogues of the companies with which they are associated), and unlike such pioneering ventures as the paper bound Gramophone Shop Encyclopedias of 1930 and 1931, the present work carries this principle a step beyond an arrangement by composers to a presentation of each composer's discography work by work, with complete recorded versions of each composition in its original form followed immediately by clearly indicated recorded excerpts, transcriptions or arrangements, and—in the case of vocal works—performances in translated versions. . . .

' To bring order to the chaos of languages found on record labels and in existing catalogues, we have used the original language for listing all titles and texts in English, French, German, Italian and Spanish. Those in such less generally familiar languages as Hungarian, Russian, Polish, Bohemian, the Scandinavian tongues, etc, are catalogued in English whenever English translations are available. However, in all cases where a title or text is widely known (or given record labelling) in more than one language, translations are provided. In addition, cross-references to the principal listing will be found under the more familiar translated titles.

' (One of our primary aims has been to avoid the inconsistency of

existing lists as exemplified by the appearance—in the same catalogue
—of one recording of *La Valse* by Ravel under " Valse " and another
under " Waltz ", or the far more involved and confusing presentation
—in a recent Bach list—of recorded chorale-preludes as " *Das alte
Jahr* " (under " D "), " *Farewell I Gladly Bid Thee,*" " *Jésus Christ
était dans son suaire,*" and so on through whatever and as many
languages as the various recordings chance to bear on their labels.)

' The scheme of arrangement may be grasped perhaps most readily
by examining first a table of the various essential factors included and
then the explanatory notes on their treatment.

I Composers (alphabetically by surname)

a Dates, nationality, and brief identifications.

II Compositions (alphabetically by original title)

a Identification by key, opus numbers, etc.

b Medium for which the work was originally written (and original
language in the case of vocal works)

c Translations where necessary, of titles and texts

d Subdivisions, movements, etc, of larger works; individual excerpts
from operas.

III Recorded Performances

a Artist or performing organization

b Record make, order number, size, list price

c Number of record sides and/or coupled selection

d Language of vocal works (if other than the original)

e Accompaniments (if other than orchestral)

f Additional—European—order numbers for recordings pressed in
various countries under more than one label.

' The whole system of arrangement is based upon an organization of
these factors so as to secure the maximum conciseness compatible with
clarity.'

INDEX

In this index all definite and indefinite articles have been dropped. Similarly, accents do not appear in the index, and this has been done purely in the interest of typographical clarity. Books are indexed under title, the author's name only being indexed if there is specific reference to them. Articles are indexed under the author and, in appropriate cases, subject. Journals are only indexed where the physical format is of importance to the text. The bibliographies and illustrations are not indexed. Certain abbreviations which are used freely in the text (only being identified the first time they are used) are indexed under their abbreviated form as if they were proper names. These are: ADP (automatic data processing); BIRS (British Institute of Recorded Sound); BBC (British Broadcasting Corporation); BLOWS (British Library of Wildlife Sounds); HMV (His Master's Voice); NASA (National Aeronautics and Space Administration); NCET (National Council for Educational Technology); RILM (*Répertoire International de la Littérature Musicale*); USIS (United States Information Service); and WERM (*World's Encyclopedia of Recorded Music*).

Ross, Alexander: 123
Russian names: 92
—songs: 85
Rust, Brian: 73; 121
Ryan, Milo: 80

Saint-Saens, Camille: 84
Saul, Patrick: 78
Scarlatti, Domenico: 84
Schott: 88
Schmidt-Isserstedt, Hans: 41
Schubert, Franz: 71
Schwann catalogue: 65; 78; 84; 90; 92ff; 97; 117
Scope: 33
78 Record Exchange: 27
78 RPM: 28; 38; 117
78s: 23; 56; 59; 70; 107
Shellac: 28
Ship/shore recordings: 78
Short-title entry: 50
Signing the discography: 20
Silencing material: 20
Simpson, Robert: 18; 64; 88
Six, Les: 51
Slattery, Thomas C: 11; 39
Sleeve, as source of information: 50
Slocombe, Marie: 78
Smolian, Steven: 39
Songs, Russian: 85
Sources: 84
Speciality labels: 107
Speech. 78ff
Spencer, *Sir* Charles Baldwin: 11
Spohr Society: 117
Standard bibliographic description: 50
Standard catalogue entry: 50
Standard layout: 46
Stave, Henry: 115
Steel-tape recorder: 32; 43
Stereo record guide: 89
Stereophony: 24
Stevenson, Gordon: 33
Stokowski, Leopold: 39; 51
Stratton, John: 13; 18
Stumpf, Carl: 11
Sub-entries: 47
Sullivan, *Sir* Arthur: 12
Sunday telegraph: 111
Sunday times: 111
Surfaces: 21
Systematic discography: 26

Tainter, C S: 9
Take numbers: 58
Tamagno, Francesco: 21
Tape guide: 116
Tapes: 32
Tauber, Richard: 52ff; 71
Taylor, Donald: 75
Technical quality: 44

Telegraph, high speed: 9
Tennessee archives: 80
Tennyson, Alfred Lord: 12
Theatre: 78
Thematic catalogues: 85
Theme music—treatment: 49
Theory and method in ethnomusicology: 74
Thomas, Dylan: 78
Times: 111
Tinfoil phonograph: 9
Title : 50; 51
Title, popular—arrangement by: 47
Toscanini, Arturo: 41
Transcription discs: 44
Transcripts of 78s: 52
Transliteration: 86
TV theme music: 49
Typographical style: 61

Umlaut: 58
Unidentified recordings: 49
USIS: 40

Vassar college: 99
Vaudeville: 121
Vaughan Williams, Ralph: 35, 63
—*Sixth symphony*: 41
Victor Red Seal: 21 *see also* RCA Victor
Vienna Academy of Science: 11
Vinyl: 32
Vocalion: 13; 40; 70

Wachsmann, Klaus P: 76
Walker, Malcolm: 38
Warner, Waldo: 40
Waterhouse, David: 77
Wax: 9; 40
—cylinder photograph: 11
Wear and damage: 29ff; 45
Weekly new release reporter: 117
WERM: 14; 25; 39; 40; 53; 61; 68; 71; 84
Westerlund, Gunnar: 35
Widdop, Walter: 19
Wild birds: 82
Wind music of Percy Aldrige Grainger: 11; 39
Wire recorders: 32; 43
Wildlife discographies: 81; 82; 121ff
Wolf Society: 20
Wolf, Hugo: 71
Wood, *Sir* Henry: 44
Work recorded: 59
World record club: 52
Wonder of the age: 12

Your jazz collection: 123

Zuni melodies: 11